SPIRIT OF MEXICO

BERYL MILES

Spirit of Mexico

JOHN MURRAY

FIFTY ALBEMARLE STREET

LONDON

© Beryl Miles 1961
Printed in Great Britain
by Butler & Tanner Ltd.
Frome and London

CONTENTS

1 ACROSS THE BORDER   1

2 FIRST IMPRESSIONS AND THE PEDREGAL   5

3 SAN ANGEL AND EVERY-DAY LIFE   19

4 GUADALUPE AND TEOTIHUACAN   35

5 THE MURALS OF DIEGO RIVERA   46

6 BENITO JUAREZ AND JESUS URUETA   58

7 ANTONIO'S WEDDING   70

8 TO OAXACA AND CHIAPAS   94

9 PAPANTLA AND THE VANILLA GODDESS   119

10 GOOD FRIDAY AT IXTAPALAPA   130

11 ARTS AND CRAFTS OF CENTRAL MEXICO   136

12 TULA AND CHOLULA   147

13 GUANAJUATO AND THE PLAYS   160

14 THE RAINY SEASON; NOGALES AND MONTE ALBAN   179

15 CHIHUAHUA   191

GLOSSARY   201

INDEX   205

[vii]

ACKNOWLEDGEMENTS

I AM so grateful to all those who helped me during my stay in Mexico, and especially to the following:

Margarita Urueta for her great kindness and help; His Excellency Pablo Campos Ortiz; Dr. Alfonso Caso; John H. Grepe of Libreria Britanica; Norman Pelham Wright; Licenciado Enrique Ruelas Espinosa and his actors of Guanajuato; Dr. Villa ROJAS of the Instituto Nacionel Indigenista of San Cristóbal de las Casas, also Señor Dorres; Mercedes and Carlos Tejeda; Martina Barrioz Alvarez of Chihuahua; Jaime Jones of Puebla; the Mexican Tourist Office, and Señor Rodriguez and to Helen O'Gorman for her Mexican Flower Calendar.

I also wish to thank Sir John Taylor of the British Mexican Society in London, Cottie A. Burland, Kenneth Bannister and Catherine Sills for their help.

A special Thank you goes to William Deneen for so many delightful journeys in the station-wagon; to my father for being a most willing 'reader'; and to Olive Norman for endless cups of tea while I was typing the manuscript.

BERYL MILES

BOOKS OF REFERENCE

Conquest of Mexico   W. H. Prescott
The Aztecs of Mexico   G. C. Valliant
Portrait of Mexico   Bertram D. Wolfe
Mexican Kaleidoscope   Norman Pelham Wright
Intercambio   Organ of the British Chamber of Commerce in
  Mexico
Made in Mexico   Patricia F. Ross
Diego Rivera's Frescoes   R. S. Silva E.

CHAPTER I

ACROSS THE BORDER

I<small>T WAS THREE O'CLOCK</small> in the morning and I stood in the moonlight in a narrow street of Laredo on the Texas-Mexican border after the first half of my three thousand five hundred-mile bus journey from New York to Mexico City. Though it was only the first days of January it was like a June night, yet only two days before I had been shivering in a snow blizzard on my way through West Virginia, and when I had left England a week earlier it had been in a December gale. There was no bus out of Laredo till the morning and the seat in the bus station had grown too hard to sleep on any longer. When I wandered in again the Border Patrol Officer, whose duty it was to guard this part of the frontier, shifted his revolver a trifle so that he could lean up more comfortably against the counter, glad to have someone to talk to.

'It was about this time in the morning in '54 when the river rose,' he commented reflectively. 'Must have been about ten inches of rain—they lost half the population on the Mexican side. It's a bad river here—fifty feet deep in places, then suddenly there's a rock seam where it's only knee-deep. Some guys know the crossings; others sit all afternoon working it out. Sometimes as many as six or seven bodies get washed up at a time.'

'What do you do with them?' I asked curiously.

'Well, unless there's some identification—or a knife in the back —we just bury them on the bank. It's like face powder—loose, easy to dig. You can put a crop of cotton in and it will grow! It's a long border—over a thousand miles. Must be a graveyard by now—and no markers! It's mostly smuggling *marihuana*' he went on—'looks rather like a fern. Smoked in cigarettes, it makes a man three times as strong! The other thing is heroin. Whenever we seize a big lot it's through information. Some guy who wants to get rich pulls out of the racket and retires after making a secret deal with us. It's not always smugglers,' he added, 'often it's illegal immigrants—"wet backs" we call them. Hundreds of Mexicans come over here every year as *braceros* (agricultural labourers), work in the fields in Texas in the winter and leave again in the spring.'

With the first light of dawn he got into his patrol car; then, taking out his wallet, he pulled out a card and handed it to me.

'Ring me if you're in trouble,' he said, and with a wave he drove off. I glanced down at the card; it said 'Laredo Secret Police'.

The bus arrived at six o'clock, and at the Migration Office down the road we were shepherded into an ill-lit hall where an official typed out our particulars awkwardly with four fingers on an antiquated machine. For the next quarter of an hour the room was a chaotic scene as owners of suitcases knelt on them, and others wrestled with bulging cardboard boxes, or baskets; someone obligingly came and sat on my cases for me.

Once across the International Bridge over the Rio Grande River, with its innocent-looking banks, we were in Mexico. Here sweet sellers in shabby straw hats or shawls were squatting on the pavements with their wares, but once we left the town behind we ran straight into the desert, a stony wilderness in which the highway stretched endlessly into the horizon. Vegetation was mainly clumps of *nopal* cactus (prickly pear), the most common of the Mexican cacti of which many are edible, leaf, flower and fruit. There were also a few stiff-looking *yucca* trees, but most astonishing were the *mesquite* bushes whose feathery foliage held all the ethereal greenness of an English spring. In the distance were mountains but there was no sign of life apart from an occasional box-like earth dwelling.

An approaching bus was a tiny speck in the distance, and as we drew nearer both drivers waved and shouted at each other, then screeched to a standstill. They jumped out, embraced fondly, and exchanged some papers. Spanish was being spoken all round me now in the bus, though too fast for me to understand much. However, thanks to the record course which I had been pursuing ardently for the last few months, I could identify a phrase or two, which made me feel remarkably pleased with myself.

It was fifty miles before we halted again for what the driver announced as our 'meal stop'. Most of the houses in the village, though now in a sad state of dilapidation, had obviously known better times and more paint. The sun beat down from a cloudless sky; it was extremely hot and I decided to retire to the cloakroom and change into a summer dress before I had a meal.

This pleasant dream was quickly dispelled. The 'cloakroom' was simply a converted pigsty in the back yard. Even the meal was denied me for in locating this 'cloakroom' I had passed through the kitchen where, from a dirty wooden table, a freshly skinned kid covered in flies stared up at me glassy-eyed; the remains of its predecessor, garnished with onion and tomato, was to be our 'meal'. A banana and a packet of dry biscuits was the most I managed from *that* restaurant—and I retired into the street with those.

In an adjoining patio where scarlet bougainvillea tumbled down peeling plaster walls, a green parrot, which had been screaming out some Spanish not in my record course, let out a penetrating wolf-whistle at the sight of me, or perhaps just my banana.

As it grew noticeably hotter, the driver did some surreptitious fiddling with the air-conditioning which should have been working, but we soon realized that for the next twenty-four hours we should all have to make do with the one small fan which was feebly stirring the air around his head.

That afternoon we reached Monterrey, familiar only because I remembered that something had 'happened' in Monterrey—but that I knew had been 'a long time ago' when stars and guitars were the main source of entertainment, whereas now the inhabitants of Monterrey, numbering over three hundred and forty thousand, have a choice of nineteen cinemas to occupy their evenings and over six hundred industries to keep them busy in the daytime. Due to the fact that the mountains here are full of minerals it is now the third largest industrial city in Mexico.

However, half an hour later, neither Monterrey nor its nineteen cinemas might have existed, for there was only a stony wilderness again, though now mountains sprawled along the horizon like elongated caterpillars.

By evening everyone in the bus was chattering to each other and I was venturing to try out my newly-acquired Spanish for the first time. As sunset softened down the harsh hot outlines of stones and cactus and the mountains were pinpointed in rose against a sky of duck-egg green, two girls began to sing in harmony. Soon all the passengers had joined in, as well as both drivers. They all sang with complete unselfconsciousness.

The spare driver leaned across to me.

'You like our singing, señorita?'

'It's lovely!' I exclaimed.

'I will tell them. They will be pleased!' and standing up in the aisle he announced that the señorita from England had much enjoyed the singing. Everyone began to clap.

'You must stand up,' he urged. 'They want to see you!'

As I stood up and bowed as gracefully as the swaying bus would permit there was more clapping; then the singing began again with renewed vigour.

'Now they are singing a special song for *you*, señorita!' exclaimed the driver delightedly.

With darkness the bus gradually subsided into silence as people settled down to try and get some sleep, since we were not due in Mexico City until two in the morning.

It was nearer three than two when we did arrive. The foyer of the hotel, though dimly lit as befitted the hour, was ornate with heavy carving, and my bedroom, with its tiled bathroom, hot water and fluffy towels, was as luxurious as this elaborate foyer secretly led me to hope it might be—though since the episode of the kid with the glassy eyes I had been a little uncertain what to expect.

CHAPTER 2

FIRST IMPRESSIONS AND THE PEDREGAL

IT WAS EXCITING to wake to brilliant sunshine, to be putting on a summer dress and sandals in January. The hotel was far too expensive for more than one night, so my first job was to find a cheap room. I found one in Calle Lerma and moved into it right away.

As I was unpacking, a scrap of paper dropped to the floor. I picked it up; it was the address of a Señora Margarita Urueta in a part of Mexico City called San Angel. It had come into my possession in rather an odd way. A few days before leaving England I had passed a bookshop where they were displaying the works of Rudolf Steiner, and went in to see if they could get me a certain volume before I left for Mexico.

'How strange!' exclaimed the owner. 'A lady from Mexico was here half an hour ago—also to buy a book of Steiner's.' He picked up a scrap of paper. 'Here's her address! Why not take it? You might come across her. It *is* rather a coincidence!'

I had put the paper in my pocket and forgotten about it—now here it was. I looked at it again . . . it *was* rather a coincidence. On the spur of the moment I sat down and wrote a note to Señora Urueta explaining how I came to have her address, and suggesting that if she was in town one day perhaps we could meet and have coffee together. Then I went out to explore.

Running off Calle Lerma were little streets with Spanish-style houses of pink or pale green plaster, with lovely wrought-iron doors. What struck me most after the arid country I had passed through in the north were the number of trees in the streets, and the grass verges. There was a continual scent of hot wet earth as gardeners, in wide straw hats and faded blue overalls, played their hoses on thick coarse grass. A man walked up to one of them, borrowed his hose for a minute, put his face and his head under it, then, with a bow, handed it back and went on his way shaking the water out of his hair.

Just round the corner I found a magnificent avenue—Paseo de la Reforma, Mexico City's main thoroughfare, over eight miles long. This part of it runs almost entirely between trees, mostly ash and eucalyptus, and many were already in leaf; at intervals, on the grass verges beneath them, bronze urns alternated with small bronze statues of Mexican heroes or statesmen, and every so often Reforma widened into a Circle with a monument. The one with a slender gold angel poised perilously on the top of a tall marble column was the Independence Monument; during the earthquake of 1957 the original angel lost her balance and finished up in pieces on the ground, so this is Angel No. 2. Inside the column itself are the remains of famous heroes of the Revolution for Independence.

People were sitting about on wide stone seats, often with a barefooted boy in a ragged shirt polishing their shoes, putting the polish on neatly with his fingers; a *peso* is the usual price for a shoeshine. I soon found that you had only to sit down on a park seat for one or more shoeshine boys to appear like magic.

There was an endless stream of traffic, for Reforma leads out of the city, through Chapultepec Park—Mexico's Hyde Park, with its Castle, boating lake and Zoo—and on to the expensive residential district of Lomas (Little Hills) with its modern pseudo-Spanish villas.

Afterwards I followed Reforma in the opposite direction. Where it makes a junction with Insurgentes, the longest street in the city, over nine miles long, was the magnificent statue of Cuauhtémoc, the last Aztec Emperor, splendid in plumed helmet and cape. Beyond this, Reforma lost that 'country' look and turned into an imposing avenue of skyscrapers, hotels and shops.

At the Plaza de la Reforma, with its bronze equestrian statue of

Charles IV of Spain, Avendida Juárez went off at right angles, and, half-way down it I was again walking among lawns, trees and fountains, this time of Alemada Park, where, on blue and yellow-tiled seats, Indians in their dark-patterned *zarapes* (woven rectangular blankets with a slit for the head) were staring meditatively at the splashing water or the passers-by, or dozing, head on chest, their hats tipped over their eyes. Beyond the row of tall palms that fringe the park stood Bellas Artes—the Palace of Fine Arts; in the brilliant sunlight its marble walls and domes looked as if they might be made of sugar. Built to commemorate the One Hundredth Anniversary of Mexican Independence, it houses the Art Collection and the main theatre with its unique drop-curtain of about a million pieces of iridescent glass forming a painted mosaic of the Valley of Mexico. This shows the two famous snow-capped volcanoes, Popocatépetl and Ixtaccíhuatl, whose pronunciation is a trial and trouble to almost every visitor, for the former (Po-po-kah-TAY-petl) is not nearly so simple as it looks, while the latter (Eesh-tahk-SEE-hwahtl) defeats you even before you begin. 'Popo', as it is known affectionately to the Mexicans, is covered in perpetual snow, and on Columbus Day, 12th October, there is a special mountain-climbing expedition, and a celebration on the edge of the crater. The last official eruption was in 1802, although in 1922 there were symptoms of extra internal heat which somewhat diminished the perpetual snow. The glass curtain was painted by Mexico's famous landscape and volcano painter, Dr. Atl. Every Sunday morning it is subtly illuminated so that you can witness all the grandeur of dawn and sunrise over the Valley from a comfortable seat and at no cost.

From Bellas Artes the real shopping centre spreads out in all directions, and I began to make my way up Avendida Francisco I. Madero, Mexico's Bond Street, where there were magnificent displays of silver and leather—two of Mexico's main products. There were miniature Mexican hats, pairs of fighting cocks, and silver-studded saddles for the *charro* (skilled and wealthy horsemen) who ride in Chapultepec Park on Sundays. Considering the exquisite workmanship, and that most articles were hand-made, things were not expensive. Madero was so narrow, and so over-powered by its tall buildings, that whilst one pavement was in deep shade, and consequently crowded with shoppers, the other was in burning sunshine and almost empty.

The incessant flow of traffic—mostly cars and coloured taxis—was interrupted by traffic lights at each intersection, where sellers of lottery tickets, newspapers or feather dolls on strings, waited to dart like minnows towards the open car windows.

As ninety per cent of the city's oldest colonial buildings are in this area, lovely curved façades of pink *tezontle* volcanic stone rose up incongruously above displays of television sets or exclusive gowns.

Men, meeting on the pavement, would embrace each other affectionately. I noticed that though the men all wore hats I never saw a woman in one though the sun was beating down. Women of the poorer classes, almost all of whom had their black hair in two smooth plaits, all wore *rebozos* (long black speckled shawls) thrown over head and shoulders; all the others were bareheaded, unless they were going into a church, when they would produce a small black lace veil from their handbags. This absence of hats emphasized the predominance of black hair among Mexican women; I rarely saw a blonde or brown head among the crowds unless it was a visitor.

Madero ended so abruptly that it was like coming out of a tunnel into bright light to find oneself suddenly projected into the vast bare sunlit expanse of the *zocalo*, an enormous paved square with traffic circling it continuously. Once, this was another oasis of trees and grass, but as the population of the city increased and the traffic doubled itself—there are now over twelve thousand taxis—it was decided that more freedom of movement was needed at this focal point, especially for parades, for the *zocalo* is right on the doorstep of the National Palace which takes up one whole side of it. So, to the distress of many, trees and grass were removed. It is from the central doorway of the Palace that every road in the Republic starts to reckon its kilometres.

Another side of the square was occupied by the Cathedral which was massive and rather gloomy. From it a smell of cold incense drifted out on to the hot air.

My two outstanding impressions of Mexico City at the end of that first day were that Mexican traffic, especially the taxis, was the most hectic I had ever seen, and that all male Mexicans seemed to have a small black moustache.

I was just going out to continue my explorations next morning when there was a knock at the door and a cry of '*Teléfono, señorita!*'

I went out on to the landing where the telephone hung next to a huge glass jar in a swinging metal frame—the *agua purificada* (purified drinking water) supplied free for the use of tenants, since the ordinary tap water is undrinkable.

'Good morning,' said a pleasant voice in English. 'This is Margarita Urueta. I have just received your note. Could you come over to my house for coffee this morning? San Angel is about forty minutes out of town, but you can get one of those cream trolley buses at the statue of Cuauhtémoc—I expect you have seen that already. It is our good landmark! It is not far to walk when you leave the tram.' She laughed—I liked the sound of her laugh. 'I am sure being English you like walking! *Adios.* I look forward to meeting you.'

The trolley bus was a great improvement on most buses I had seen so far—small shabby affairs which rattled along as if they were about to fall to pieces. Beside the driver was a little wooden slab with slots in it to hold the different sized coins, like some complicated game of shove-halfpenny.

Mexican currency was not difficult to master. A hundred *centavos*, in coins ranging from one to fifty, made one *peso* (the first denomination in paper money, and worth 7*d*.); after that there were notes worth five, ten, twenty-five or a hundred *pesos*.

Soon we branched off from Insurgentes into Avendida Revolucíon which runs parallel to it towards the outskirts of the city where San Angel lies. At the traffic lights a boy jumped on crying, '*Chicle! Chicle!*'; this plaintive cry, announcing the sale of chewing gum, goes on somewhere within hearing nearly all day like a stuck gramophone record.

In the narrow main street of San Angel, shops were like small dark caves, and the pavements were broken and dusty. Women squatting on the ground wrapped in their *rebozos* were selling pumpkin seeds, also sweets and custards from smeared glass cases like little aquariums.

The road I was looking for turned out to be a cobbled lane between high grey stone walls. It ended in a small clearing of coarse grass and towering eucalyptus trees, but there were no houses to be seen, nothing but more high walls. In the longest of these, however, was a huge wrought-iron gate and I found it bore the number of Señora Urueta's house. When I rang, a brown-faced Mexican with sandalled feet unbarred the gate and pointed towards a large white house standing in the gravelled courtyard. The heavy front door, also of wrought-iron, was opened by a short dark-haired woman in a white apron; a sturdy boy of about two clung to her skirt, his feet slipping on the highly polished hall; above hung a glittering chandelier.

I was shown into a magnificent high-ceilinged library, one end of which was taken up by a vast casement window behind which scarlet paper-thin petals of bougainvillea pressed themselves on to the glass. On a long polished table stood some large object over which was draped what appeared to be a richly embroidered altar cloth.

Books lined all the walls apart from one space taken up by a wide stone fireplace, and another over a deep blue sofa where there hung a more than life-size painting of a woman with a cloud of dark hair. Her chin was propped up in her hands, and her deeply brooding eyes stared straight down into mine. A flight of stone stairs with a wrought-iron balustrade ran up to a gallery; at that moment light footsteps sounded on the stairs and I found myself looking up into the identical pair of eyes, only this time they were smiling and friendly. This was Margarita Urueta.

We sat on the sofa under her portrait (which I discovered later was by Siqueros, the famous Mexican painter—one of his best), and began to talk—of Rudolf Steiner's philosophy which had so strangely brought us together . . . of her visit to London . . . of my visit to Mexico.

Margarita was a writer and a playwright—one of her plays was just about to be produced in Mexico City. The embroidered 'altar cloth' turned out to be a white *toreo* cape offered to her at a famous *corrida* (bullfight) and it was covering her typewriter!

An hour had passed before we realized it.

'Oh, how nice it has been discussing all these things—and in English!' she exclaimed. 'What talks we could have if you lived here!' She stopped. 'You are staying in Mexico for seven or eight months—and I have plenty of room. Could you not live here instead of the hotel? Then when we were not both busy we could go on talking! You could buy what you want in the market and Mina could prepare it for you. You could go off and see Mexico and come back here, and we could carry on our discussions where we left off! Isn't that a splendid idea?'

I agreed that it certainly was.

'Why not come right away?' she went on. 'This evening if you like. How is your Spanish by the way? Mina speaks no English—but you will soon get used to speaking Spanish!'

She came out with me into the bright sunlight of the gravelled courtyard.

'Here in San Angel we have much belonging to our earliest civilizations,' she said, 'the Pedregal, a whole desert of lava, and Cuicuilco, our oldest pyramid. Oh, I will show you many things! We have an expression in Mexico,' she added as we shook hands; 'you will hear it often when you say goodbye at a Mexican home: "*Es su casa*"—"This is your house." Usually it is not to be taken literally—it is politeness; but this time it has the real meaning—this *is* your house! I shall tell Mina to expect you tonight and we will see each other tomorrow.'

As I retraced my steps down that narrow cobbled alley I was still a little dizzy with the swift turn of events.

Evening found me returning, this time in an orange taxi and with my cases. Once more the gate was unbarred for me and I stood at the front door, but this time in the lamplight from the courtyard; behind me stretched a belt of shadows that was the garden. The house was in darkness. I rang twice; there was still no response. Suddenly I wondered whether the whole thing, from the piece of paper with the address on it, to my meeting with Margarita and my present appearance on the dark step, might not perhaps be part of a dream—'in which case,' I said to myself, 'it's high time I woke up!'

However, at that moment there was a heavy sound of bolts being drawn and the door swung open to reveal Mina, all smiles; behind her stood a stocky young man with a small black moustache. 'Ah, *buenas noches, señorita!*' she exclaimed, and led the way to a curving flight of stairs, while the young man shouldered my cases. Once we reached the polished landing the reason for the darkness of the house was explained; seated in a row on straw-plaited chairs in front of a television set were several servants and two boys, the older one with fair hair; the small boy who had been clinging to Mina's skirt that morning sat cross-legged on the floor. All heads were turned to watch us coming up the stairs. The fair-haired boy jumped to his feet and held out his hand.

'Good evening,' he said, speaking in slow but good English. 'I am Alfonso. My mother told me you were coming tonight. She is sorry to be out.'

In the room to which Mina now took me one whole wall was curtained and there was a long desk-like table; she pointed to it, and then to me.

'For you,' she said in Spanish, 'for your writing.' She opened a door showing a tiled bathroom. 'For you,' she repeated, then beckoned me to follow her. Downstairs in a huge kitchen a tray was already set with a jar of coffee, a cup and saucer, and a plate of the curly pastry I had seen in the bakers' shops. This, too, was for me. It was really quite overwhelming.

When I awoke next morning and pulled back the curtains I found glass doors leading out on to a balcony brilliant with sunshine and overhung with mauve bougainvillea and the feathery leaves of a jacaranda tree; lawns and trees stretched away below me.

There was a knock at the door; it was Mina; smiling, she handed me a note.

'Good morning,' I read. 'I hope you slept well. I shall be having breakfast in my room if you care to join me. Mina will show you the way.'

Margarita's room was luxurious with a rose-satin bed; she was sitting up working on a manuscript with her breakfast tray beside her; a small table with another tray stood nearby. 'I thought it was easier for Mina to give you what I have today,' she said.

There was a glass of fresh orange and pineapple juice, a large slice of papaya (like a melon, with yellow skin and orange flesh) over which we squeezed the juice of tiny green limes; afterwards there were sweet pastries.

'I have to go to the University this morning to collect some books from the library,' said Margarita as we sipped our coffee. 'Would you like to come with me? Our University is something quite unusual. I'll get Mina to put a folding table in your room later,' she added, 'you may like to take some of your meals on your balcony. That is the joy of Mexico City. We are so high up on this Central Plateau—7,233 feet—that it never gets too hot like some parts of Mexico. You came through some of that desert country of the north in the bus. It is best to go slowly at first up at this altitude; many people feel they have no energy, others feel the opposite—all on edge. If you feel like that it is good to relax in the swimming pool!'

She pointed across her balcony, and I caught a glimpse through the trees of blue water among the green lawns. (Now I knew I really *was* having a dream!)

One interesting thing about living at that altitude is that low blood-pressure people feel very happy, because their blood pressure goes up to normal, whereas high blood-pressure people often have to retire to sea level.

'Is it as warm as this all the time?' I asked. Margarita shook her head.

'I hope you have warm things with you as well as summer things. You nearly always want a jacket in the evenings, though we have not that big difference between summer and winter that you have in England. Our difference is really between the dry season from November to June, and the wet season from June to November when it rains every afternoon for about two hours—and really rains! Wait till you see it! This is our coldest time, December and January, but even then it is like summer compared to your English January! All climate in Mexico depends on whether the land is low-lying, when it is hot and tropical; or far away from the sea and high, when it is cooler.'

I was sitting on my balcony in the sunshine later that morning when Margarita called up that she was leaving for the University.

It was only about ten minutes away yet it was like going into another world, for it lay among the strange black and bronze wilderness of the Pedregal, or Lava Field, which closed us in so suddenly that it was as if San Angel and Mexico City did not exist. Margarita pointed to a range of mountains and a distant peak.

'Over there is Ajusco, one of the volcanoes that made the Pedregal,' she said, pulling up the car so that we could look across the great horizontal ridges that layered the landscape for miles on both sides of the road, relieved only by clusters of dry yellow grass, and feathery pepper trees with drooping clusters of pink berries.

As we drove deeper into the Pedregal, strange buildings began to appear. One gigantic multicoloured structure, like an upended box, its façade glittering with mosaic work of hundreds of pieces of coloured stone, was the University Library.

'It was made by our architect, John O'Gorman,' said Margarita. 'He lives in San Angel and is a good friend of mine. It is his masterpiece. He sent all over Mexico to find those stones—he has woven into it all the Indian symbols. Over a hundred architects worked to create this University—it is unlike any other in the world. In Mexico people are either for or against it because it cost so much to build.'

In avenues feathered with pepper trees signposts of yellow mosaic pointed out the Faculties, many of which were also decorated with gigantic coloured mosaics. The enormous sports stadium, which holds a hundred thousand, was built of the same *adobe* bricks which the Indians use for their homes.

'The only trouble is that since they moved the University out here it has made it very difficult for the teaching staff,' said Margarita. 'It was right in the centre of the town before, and as most of our Professors work at something else because the salary is not large—most are lawyers, doctors, or Government officials —it is a long way for them to come, so many classes only start in the evening. Mexico City uses the University City as a sort of playground at the weekends; many people drive out here for picnics.'

When we left the University, Margarita continued on up the road.

'While we are so close I want to show you Cuicuilco, the oldest pyramid on the American Continent,' she said.

A rough track led us to a huge circular mound, sixty feet high, that looked as if it had pushed its way through the lava.

'It is not exactly a pyramid, though we call it so,' explained Margarita. 'It is a flat-topped cone—three inside one really, because it was used by more than one archaic civilization as their place of worship.'

There had been no roof, only an altar, on top. Earth and sky, priest and people—who gazed up in silence from the foot of the mound—had been as one unit, anticipating by several thousand years Browning's,

> 'Why, where's the need of Temple, when the walls
> O' the world are that?'

Instead of a stairway there was a steep earth incline, and from the top we looked right across that vast wilderness of petrified cross-currents.

'But to get the feeling of Cuicuilco you must know what happened in the Valley of Mexico even earlier,' said Margarita. 'Men were living first by hunting. At Tepexpan on the other side of the city they found the remains of a hunter buried in an ancient swamp; he had been spearing a mammoth and its remains were there also. When they used the carbon test they found he had died over nine thousand years ago!'

But by the time archaic man had settled around Cuicuilco he was already growing maize. As he had no domestic animals to eat up the leaves these piled up all round his home, and, luckily for the archeologists, all his broken pottery and tools became embedded in the rubbish like currants in a cake. Some of those rubbish beds had taken six or seven hundred years to accumulate and in them archeologists also found human remains embedded, since it had been easier, with wooden tools, to dig graves in that soft surface. Three times archaic man of those Middle Cultures who lived on this site, now known as the Pedregal, and worshipped here at Cuicuilco, was engulfed by burning lava—first from the volcano Xictli, later from Ajusco. By using the carbon-14 test on the stratas of refuse, which are revealed in layers when the ground is sliced vertically, scientists have discovered that pottery embedded beneath one of the lava flows dates back to 1200 B.C. The name Cuicuilco means 'A Place for Singing and Dancing' and the pyramid is thought to have been used for the worship of the Fire God, the oldest of the gods—certainly a fitting Divinity for such an explosive region.

'It is good to come out here sometimes and think of these things,' remarked Margarita reflectively. 'It makes many small personal problems go back into their right perspective! It is good that you have seen Cuicuilco first,' she added as we drove back towards San Angel, 'for after it came all our other great cultures —Teotihuacán with its Pyramid of the Sun; Tula, the great capital of the Toltecs; and Tenochtitlan, the city of the Aztecs. Having seen Cuicuilco first, your feet are on solid ground!'

Where the Pedregal stopped abruptly and the houses of San Angel began, Margarita swung to the left.

'You saw what man did here *before* the lava flow came. I will show you what he is doing with it now that it *is* here—though you saw already something of that with the University.' She pointed to a long wall. 'In there is the home of John O'Gorman, the architect of the Library. *His* house is a real cave formed by the lava. Now, here are what we call the Gardens of the Pedregal.'

We turned into an avenue from which roads wound off in all directions. All were named after the natural elements; the main ones had names like Avenue of the Fountains, Boulevard of the Light; smaller ones were Hail, Dew, Clouds, Snow, Headland, Slate, Cascade, Rain, Fissure, Outcropping of a Vein, and so on. Your postal address if you lived in the Gardens of the Pedregal might be simply 43 Water, 29 Cloud, or 50 Snow.

Each house was set down on a section of natural lava which had been used to create an original garden. Ponds and tiny lawns had been coaxed into every hollow like small glistening jewels; everything followed the natural contour, however fantastic, of the lava flow. Needless to say there were rockeries without equal. Most of the houses were set up on stilts, either back or front, to allow for their irregular foundations, but all were the last word in modern design, sometimes the whole front being just a single sheet of glass; many even had a swimming pool among the rocks. Apart from the flowers—pink geraniums, blue plumbago, forsythia—which had been 'imported', everything else, even the roads, was of volcanic stone. It was as if the dreams of ancient man, imprisoned for thousands of years within the lava, had emerged and crystallized into form.

'It was a young Mexican landscape gardener, Luis Barragan, who first thought of building homes out here,' said Margarita. 'He had built many artificial grottoes and rockeries for rich people in the city, and one day, walking in the Pedregal, he thought how much easier it would be to build such things where the rock already was than to take it somewhere else. So, for very little money, because nobody had ever thought of such a thing, he bought a section, and put up a sample house. It was immediately a success. Now it is considered very fashionable to live on the Pedregal. Some of our richest and most notable people, artistic ones especially, live in these homes. Many people buy a vacant lot as a speculation because you can always sell it for more.'

On one plot which had just been sold, piles of stone had been chipped off ready for building. It must be rather nice when you buy your plot to know that it includes enough building stone for the house and the garden walls; and that even that, when removed, scarcely makes any impression on what remains for your rockeries.

So ended my first introduction to the Pedregal, the strange link between two ages, where, almost simultaneously, one may delve down with one hand into Mexico's remotest past, and with the other, reach up and touch the peak of her 'today'.

I came back to it many times during the months that followed. I would find some natural seat below a ridge of rock and sit there picturing the red molten mass pouring down the sides of the volcano and moving slowly over the valley. The top layer would already be blackened by the time it reached where I was sitting, though underneath it would still be glowing, and the moving molten mass pushing it on relentlessly from behind would force it over and over into these twisted shapes of black and bronze that lay all round me.

Often I would come here to watch the sunset, for as the rays fanned out in golden shafts over the tortured wilderness it was like witnessing the primordial stirrings of a universe.

However, I did not linger too long once the sun had set. I remembered something Margarita had said: 'Never come here after dark. It is not a good place. Many thieves come here to hide at nightfall—we call them The Thieves of the Pedregal!'

CHAPTER 3

SAN ANGEL AND EVERY-DAY LIFE

S O BEGAN LIFE in San Angel, and there was so much to do and see that for a time I felt no inclination to wander further afield. Down every narrow cobbled lane I would come upon perfect examples of sixteenth-century Spanish architecture, for this had been one of the favourite villages for a country residence in Colonial days.

Many of these old houses had been completely modernized inside; some had solar heaters on the roof whereby the water, heated all day under glass by the sun, was finally passed through an electric heater which worked automatically if it was not hot enough. However, the huge wooden doors were still set with iron studs, the windows shadowed by wrought-iron grills, and impenetrable stone walls still encompassed their grounds. Yet I knew now that behind those walls lay gardens of unbelievable loveliness, though often nothing betrayed them but the tips of tall trees, or an escaping tendril of scarlet from some hidden cascade of blossom. Through an open gate I would sometimes get a glimpse, even though it was only January, of a mingling of roses and carnations, of poppies, mimosa or oleander, as well as showers of yellow jasmine and pale blue plumbago. Once I saw bronze wallflowers, though there seemed to be no bulbous plants like daffodils or tulips.

I would sit in one of the little plazas, where the trees interlaced across red sandy paths and grubby barefooted children balanced on the rim of the empty stone fountain. Rackety second-class buses, grey or fawn, would come grinding up the steep cobbled street into San Angel, packed so tightly that passengers bulged out of doors and windows. By contrast the long creamy-coloured trolleys glided up smoothly and easily, rarely overcrowded, for their charge was forty *centavos* (about 3*d.*) into town—double the fare of the second-class bus.

Occasionally an orange taxi, or a green one with a black and white tooth pattern—nicknamed *cocodrilo* (crocodile) by the Mexicans—would come rushing up the hill, skidding recklessly on the cobbles, menacing the leisurely-moving straw-hatted old men with their white cloth bundles, and the women with their long black plaits, and babies wound into their black *rebozos*. (Those babies looked so comfortable, as if they were sitting up in a little armchair, that I soon felt sorry for any baby I saw dangling awkwardly unsupported by a *rebozo*.)

There were always shoe-cleaners, boys and men, at work, their patched cotton trousers secured with string or worn leather belts, their hair falling into their eyes as they polished the shoes of compatriots often as shabby as themselves; when unoccupied they sat on their shoe-cleaning boxes and read the old newspaper or magazine which they kept handy for their clients.

San Angel, known to the Aztecs as Chimalistac, was given its present name by the Spaniards who Christianized as many of the Indian names as quickly as possible; but after the Revolution, when the State broke away from the Church, it was, so to speak, 'unchristened', and became 'Villa Obregón' after General Alvaro Obregón. However, most of the residents, being Catholics, refused to change the name, so San Angel it still remains, except for the postal address which is firmly 'Villa Obregón'.

Now and then, bells would chime out from the old Convent with its multi-coloured domes. It is now a museum, as all convents and monasteries were closed during the Revolution.

I remember the time I went across to explore its dim pillared cloisters. The guide kindly lent me his torch and directed me down a shadowy flight of steps into the crypt. There the flickering light picked out, one by one, the nuns of San Angel, still in their crumbling best, propped up in glass coffins, their skulls still cowled and the toes of their shoes falling away.

Afterwards I wandered through the echoing stone cloisters and pushed open the creaking doors of the small numbered cells, with their heavily shuttered windows. I could not resist lying down for a moment on the hard plank bed to see exactly what No. 58 would have seen as she lay there. The main thing I noticed, before the little log of wood which had served her as a pillow rolled away from under my head, was her Penance Whip hanging behind the door—a delicate little affair of seven strands of chain.

Just down the corridor was a room labelled 'Tribune', and through a long grill at one end I found myself looking directly down on to the High Altar of the Church of San Angel. This was how the nuns had attended Mass unobserved.

On the next occasion I was there quite a few people were also wandering round as it was a *fiesta* day. One girl slipped on the stone stairs, sprained her ankle and fainted. She was carried to a corner and propped up on a chair. When dipping a handkerchief in the fountain proved ineffectual, the porter produced a jug and poured the water over her head, then down her neck, following it up with the huge cold key of the crypt. He then rubbed whisky over her head and face till she smelt like a raving alcoholic, while an onion, cut in two, was held under her nose and a bunch of herbs, hastily gathered in the garden, waved over her. This combined shock treatment finally brought her to.

Not far from the Convent, on Insurgentes, was the monument to General Alvaro Obregón, with a bronze statue of him showing his arm cut off at the elbow, a casualty he had suffered at the Battle of Celaya. The inscription read 'To General Alvaro Obregón at the place of his Sacrifice'; on this spot had stood the Restaurant Bombilla in which he was assassinated.

What fascinated me most, I think, were the markets, and I explored them all in turn. I never ceased to be amazed at the profusion of flowers. Old battered dried-milk tins would hold some exotic flowering cactus—the sort you can keep on your window-sill in England for years, cherish it like a child, and never be rewarded by so much as a bud. Yet these, covered in blossom, were selling for a couple of shillings. Great masses of gladioli and arum lilies in every pastel shade were heaped up into solid banks of blossom. Most of these are grown out at Xochimilco (where flower-decorated boats ply up and down the canals on Sundays) and brought into the city, literally by the ton, every morning.

In San Angel, the unpretentious little café which was part of the market—and to which buyers and sellers retired periodically for such things as a bowl of thick lentil soup swimming with un-cooked bananas, or just a bottled *refresco*—always had its small grubby tables weighed down with great pink and yellow spikes of left-over gladioli, top heavy in their inadequate jam jars.

On the market stalls, long poles of sugar-cane, still bearing ragged feathery leaves, were sold by the stick, or in chopped-up pieces for immediate consumption; as you chewed at the tough fibre the sweet substance oozed out leaving you with the mouth-ful of fibre to dispose of. There were piles of long flat grey pump-kin seeds with white edges, the crystallized pumpkin itself looking like a wedge of amber; glowing piles of *tuna*, the fruit of the *nopal* cactus; dozens of different sorts of chiles, from fat and bright red, to thin and pale green. (Altogether there are about fifteen different kinds so most Mexican dishes are *picante*, or 'hot with chile'.) There were mushrooms from the mountains; piles of special blue maize cobs, used for making fiesta *tortillas*; and some cobs covered with grey fungus considered a great delicacy. Lying beside the great heaps of creamy yellow maize were lumps of lime used for boiling with it to soften the skin before the maize is ground for making *masa* (dough).

There was always a queue at a nearby *tortilleria* (*tortilla* factory), a dark cave-like room opening on to the pavement. From it came the warm smell of maize dough and a sound like the clapping in a half-empty theatre as the *tortilla* maker slapped the thin round maize pancakes back and forth between her palms to flatten them before throwing them on to a huge *comal* (grill), over a charcoal fire. As soon as they were a little brown she would throw them into a large lined basket; as they accumulated someone would step out of the queue, gather up a little pile to be weighed, then wrap them up in the cloth she had brought with her, for *tortillas* must always be eaten hot. One section of every market consisted of a row of women standing behind a long trestle table, each with a basket, or zinc pail, of *tortillas* covered with a cloth to keep them warm.

The number of appetizing things which could be made with a *tortilla* was amazing. The simplest was a *sope*, a *tortilla* turned up at the edges and sprinkled with chopped raw onion; *tacos*, the most popular, were scraps of meat, tomato, raw onion and chile, rolled up in the *tortilla*, which was then fastened with a sliver of wood, or a toothpick, and fried a crispy brown. One of the least appetizing ones, to my mind, was made by an old man who sat crouched on the ground beside a heap of tiny dried fish the size of minnows, a pile of dried flies and a heap of flies' eggs, like hundreds and thousands. He would parcel a few of these together in a hot *tortilla* and they sold as fast as he could assemble them; a baby lying on the ground beside him was fed with a mouthful of flies' eggs now and again to keep it quiet. (Incidentally, flies' eggs scraped off the surface of the lake and made into a cake were considered a great delicacy by the ancient Aztecs.)

Enchilladas were *tacos*, which, instead of being fried, were cooked in a *ranchero* sauce of tomatoes, onion, garlic and chile and covered with a sauce of chopped onion, grated cheese and thick whipped sour cream. *Quesadilla* was another variety—grated cheese was mixed into the raw maize dough before the *tortilla* was made, then it was filled with meat, potatoes and beans, or the fresh yellow flowers of the *calabaza* (squash), as well as chopped chile and herbs; the edges were crimped and it was fried in deep fat. *Tamales* were just thick maize dough compounded with lard then mixed with bits of meat and chile, rolled tightly in a banana leaf, and steamed in a kerosene tin over a charcoal *brasero*; or they could be sweet instead of savoury. One stall, selling rolls and sausages, was advertising 'Hoot Doogs'.

Some of the women would blow on a *peso* for good luck as you handed it to them; others would put it to their lips and make the sign of the cross with it in order to make it double itself.

There was not often a fish stall; in fact, until recently fish was considered quite a luxury, and there were even very poor families who had never tasted it. Mexico has over six thousand miles of coastline but fishing has never been done on a really big scale. For one thing fish is a difficult thing to distribute and keep in such extremes of climate. However, the present Government, wisely deciding that they would utilize this food supply, bought up the catches of all the small scattered fishing fleets, and announced that on a certain Wednesday there would be cheap fish for all. That day over seventy tons of fish were sold in Mexico City at prices the poorest families could afford. This has been increased to two days a week and fish is now well on the way to becoming a recognized part of the Mexican diet.

There were always lots of baby chickens since most poor families buy a baby chick for a *peso* and let it wander about the one-roomed apartment, whether upstairs or down, feeding it on scraps, and keeping it for some special fiesta day.

The fruit stalls were always a splash of colour. Bananas ranged from the huge reddish plantains (cooking bananas) to the clusters of tiny sweet sugar-bananas, but you had to choose carefully, for since bananas cannot grow on the cooler region of the Plateau they are brought from the coastal regions and often picked so green that they toughen up in the cold. There were shiny dark green avocada pears—the poor man's luxury in Mexico; large yellow papaya (pawpaw); deep golden-yellow mangoes—the best, the Manilla mango, flecked with brown spots; custard apples; *mamay*, with brown tough skin, red flesh and a huge shiny black stone; and dozens of other fruits.

One section I liked especially was the 'Witches' Market' where an old wrinkled woman in a *rebozo* sat crouched on a *petate* mat among such potent charms as dried humming birds, rats, frogs and bats. She had an ancient Indian remedy for almost every ailment: magnolia syrup for paralysis; a remedy for jaundice from the leaves of the wild cotton; rue and marigold tea for washing sore eyes; an infusion of frangipani or bougainvillea for coughs; juice from the coral tree for scorpion stings; crushed dried leaves

[24]

of acacia for dressing wounds, though she strongly recommended applying cattle kidneys and toads to stop bleeding—the Indians having anticipated the discovery of adrenaline by several centuries. There were also lantana leaves to put in your ears to cure deafness; an infusion of aniseed to make your child's hair curl; or the bulb of the Jacobean lily which, if soaked in water and applied, would stop your husband's hair falling out. She also sold the large seeds of the yellow oleander—*Codo de Fraile* (Friar's Elbow)—in pairs, to be carried, one in each pocket, as a cure for haemorrhoids. However, her main stock in trade, and the one for which she had the fastest sale, were bunches of what looked like mayweed; if you had been cursed you rubbed this over yourself to remove the spell. I watched several women go away with one of these bunches hidden surreptitiously under their *rebozos*.

As you walked through the market there were always hordes of small boys begging to carry your basket. Oddly enough, though you have to keep a constant watch on your purse and pocket, you can give a laden basket to one of those boys and know that nothing will be missing; yet, if you have a car and leave it unlocked for ten minutes, you are quite liable to find everything portable gone when you come back. Some of the thieves work together, especially on the buses, where the drivers are often afraid to intervene for fear they may get a knock on the head later on their way home. I learnt my lesson very soon after my arrival. I was standing in a bus queue when I felt someone grab my wrist tightly, then, with a quick movement, he had torn my watch off and was darting through the traffic. As I went to run after him the man behind me in the queue said quickly: 'Wait here, señorita, *I* will get him for you!' and raced after him.

'What a kind man!' I thought gratefully. Unfortunately however he didn't come back—it had been *very* well arranged. I did notice then that no one else in the queue except me had been wearing a wrist-watch; in fact, I began to notice then how few people did wear one in the street.

The police, who are poorly paid, are often not much help at such moments for, since many of them have to supplement their pay by *mordidas* (bribes) you may already have been checkmated there by your opponent. Also, it is a wise policy to keep out of the hands of the police, even if you are the innocent party, since it could land you in jail until the matter is settled. One of the first pieces of advice I was given in Mexico was, 'If ever you are involved in an accident—or even see one—don't wait. Run!'

I met one man who always takes one of his houseboys in the back of the car when he goes on a journey so that if there is an accident—and they are surprisingly frequent—he need not be detained in jail himself while the thing is sorted out but the servant can go instead; the servant is not at all averse to this since his relatives can visit him and his master sees that he has plenty of food while he is there.

I soon noticed that though many shops were undeniably dirty, there were three that were always clean—banks, bakers and chemists. The banks, of which there were an amazing number, all had spacious interiors, highly polished floors and plate-glass windows, and an armed guard on duty inside; the baker (*panificadora*—quite my favourite word in Mexico) had a glass window lined with appetizing pastry-like cakes on clean shelves; while the *farmácia*, though usually open to the street, had all its drugs carefully pigeon-holed. As Mexicans have great faith in drugs with unpronounceable names there were always new ones appearing.

In the evening as I came home up the narrow streets of San Angel there would be a glimpse of a lighted billiard hall, and no matter what the time was barbers were still busy. In the city itself it was quite usual to see men having their nails manicured, sometimes by a girl with her hair done up in curlers—a head of curlers being quite a common sight in the streets and buses.

By lamplight the filigree shadows of ash and pepper tree obscured the peeling shabbiness of the plaster walls; men standing at a street corner became just white blobs of hat. Often the first intimation you had of someone approaching in those dimly lighted streets of San Angel was the white halo of a hat, for the sandalled feet made no sound on the cobbles. But, day or night, you had to keep your eyes on the pavement, for there was always something to fall into or over—some great hole that had been dug in the middle of the pavement since the morning, or the jagged block of stone that had been placed carelessly alongside to mark it, apart from which the edge of the pavement itself was frequently broken off in large lumps.

One sound that the name 'San Angel' always conjures up for me is the sound of the night watchman. He was a very old man, almost lost under an ancient hat and cape, and he would start his round about eleven o'clock, pacing the narrow streets of San Angel all night and stopping every few minutes to play a certain sequence of notes on a high-pitched flute. No matter what hour of the night I awoke, I would hear this plaintive little sound, sometimes near at hand, sometimes far away. At first I thought I should never go to sleep because of the unconscious waiting, quite against my will, for the repetition of it, but before long it was so much a part of my life at San Angel that I could not have slept without it. I found it a pathetic thought—that old man going round those dark streets playing his little flute to let the inhabitants of San Angel know that all was well because *he* was there looking after them and their property.

In addition to the night watchman there were also the combined dogs of San Angel to be reckoned with, for if the silence was broken suddenly by one staccato bark it was taken up instantly by a dozen, then by twenty. There were also the horns, for the habit of the returning owners of these large barricaded homes is to hoot for a boy to open the gate; at night, since he is probably asleep, they simply sit in their cars, with one finger on the horn, till the gate opens.

Thanks to Margarita and Mina I soon began to be familiar with many facets of everyday Mexican life. Labour is cheap, and every family with a moderate income has at least one servant; wealthier families may have a cook, two other servants, and garden boys, as well as a sewing girl and laundress who come in periodically.

Like most Mexicans, Mina took endless trouble over the preparation of her dishes, and I spent many hours in the kitchen watching her. Every morning she went off early to the market and came back laden with fruit and vegetables; she seldom bought anything tinned. Sometimes she would buy the tender new disc-like leaves of the *nopal* cactus, scrape off the sharp spines—but never wash the leaves as that makes the sticky sap ooze out. Usually she cut them in thin strips, cooked them in salty water for about twenty minutes, drained them, and finally mixed them with a sauce of pulped tomato, chopped raw onion, French dressing and a pinch of powdered marjoram; just before bringing them into the dining-room she would sprinkle grated cheese on top. She called this *nopal* relish, but I liked them even better as *nopalitos* (stuffed *nopals*). For this she would cook the leaves whole and flour them, then press two together with a thick slice of cheese between, before dipping them into beaten-up egg and frying them brown. Then she would make a rich sauce of onion, garlic, tomato and chile in the frying pan and simmer the fried stuffed *nopalitos* in it till they were thoroughly hot. They were delicious.

She seldom bought potatoes for they are expensive, being difficult to grow in Mexico owing to blight and the wet season, although they are actually native to the Americas. However, scientists have recently been experimenting with new blight-resistant varieties among Mexican farmers on the Plateau, so they may soon be eaten much more widely.

Rice, on the other hand, is an indispensable part of Mexico City's diet. A very hard-up Mexican housewife, with nothing to serve her family except boiled rice, will still 'dress it up' with one shrimp on the top, or a couple of chiles, or else mix it with a little chopped garlic and onion. Mina would do an amazing number of things with rice—apart from what she called 'Mexican style rice', which was rice either cooked whole with a few hot green chiles stuck in it, or else cooked in a brown pottery *cazuela* (cooking pot) with a little sizzling hot grease till brown. Mina then made a sauce of chopped tomato, onion and garlic with very little water, added the fried rice with a few whole green chiles, mixed it all up well, and left it on a low gas for a couple of hours, by which time the rice had swelled and filled the *cazuela*.

Apart from this there were different coloured rice dishes, all with the same basis—plain rice, washed, dried and then fried in oil with onion and garlic. For red rice, Mina would just add chicken-broth water and tomato; for black rice, bean water; for green rice, ground parsley and chicken broth; and for yellow rice, saffron; while a simple supper dish would be cooked white rice with chicken broth added, served with lumps of butter and cheese on top.

Though many Mexican dishes are *picante* many well-to-do modern Mexicans are not at all fond of hot dishes, though they all love spicy ones because there are so many herbs and spices available. One salad which Margarita often had was *guacamole*—crushed avocada pears mixed with chopped onions and herbs.

For herself, and Antonio the houseboy and the other servants, Mina would keep a pot of black beans on the stove and make plenty of *tortillas*.

One sweet she made which was very good was a sort of fruit paste of boiled crushed fruit with a lot of sugar, moulded into big squares and sliced when cold.

She did all her cooking on a large gas stove, the supply for which came from two big cylinders out in the yard; some families have a stationary gas tank and a truck comes round and fills it up every week. Most households, even if they cook on gas, keep a charcoal *brasero* (small portable charcoal oven) tucked away somewhere just in case the gas runs out, or in case they go on a pilgrimage. Marta, Margarita's daughter, who, with her husband Pepe, lived in a very modern bungalow built in a corner of her mother's garden, would sometimes send her servant over with a bowl of soup or rice to cook on our stove if her gas ran out. (Marta was usually called 'Martita' since in Mexico the diminutive 'ito' or 'ita' is added as a pet name.) Sometimes she would come running over herself to use the telephone in our kitchen. She had just acquired a new servant who had come direct from an Indian village and had never been in a town before.

'We have to speak in sign language at present,' said Marta. 'She only speaks the dialect of her village—no Spanish. At present she just laughs at everything! At home she always sleeps on the floor on a *petate* (straw) mat so she has never seen bedclothes and cannot understand about tucking them in. I'm always finding her peering round corners at me to see what I am doing. This morning I heard her tell the other maid that she had heard me talking to the dog. She found that extraordinary!'

Marta, who was trying to get her accustomed to the telephone, would come over to ring up her own house, having left the new maid stationed beside the telephone with a pencil and paper. She would then give her imaginary names and messages.

'Oh well,' she would say, 'I'd better go and see what she's made of it *this* time!'

At least it was more simple for her than it would have been a year or so earlier, for until recently Mexico had two telephone systems—a Mexican one and a Swedish one called Erikson. This meant that you had to have two different instruments; now there is only one—Mexicano. Even so, being a telephone owner in Mexico is far from simple. Firstly you must buy three thousand shares in the Telephone Company, and then may have to wait as long as three years before you get it, when you also have to pay for the testing and installation—your three thousand shares being, as it were, key money. Once you have got your telephone it is best never to move house since you cannot take it with you, neither can you officially sell your shares to the incoming tenant. You must both start all over again with another three thousand shares.

The kitchen at Margarita's was not the easiest place in the world to hold a telephone conversation, incidentally, because the green parrot, who kept Mina company from its cage beside the sink, would usually be shouting at the top of its voice, '*Perico* . . . *Perico!*' (the name for a parrot), varying this with '*Periquito*' (parakeet). At other times it would bark like the dogs, of which there were two; mew with the kittens, or even cluck like the hen, which, with a couple of baby chicks, spent the day wandering in and out of the kitchen and getting under Mina's feet. When not doing any of these things it would laugh raucously. Almost every household has one of these green parrots in the kitchen.

What to Drink

One of the first things I noticed was that Mina had no kettle—all water was boiled up in a saucepan; also, there was no teapot, since tea, except for herbal teas used as remedies, and the tea bags served in restaurants, is hardly used. Margarita always drank coffee, and Mina made hot strong chocolate for herself and the other servants, while the children drank milk. Nobody drinks the ordinary tap water, which is contaminated at the source, and I was warned straight away not to eat any salads or uncooked vegetables, or fruit that had no peel. Often when I was invited out with Margarita some delicious-looking salad would appear. Margarita would help herself, then push it discreetly past me. 'Not for you!' she would say in a low voice. The same applies to milk, unless it is pasteurized, since the water-holes at which the cattle drink are often very dirty. Most people buy the big glass jars of purified water, or else take only bottled drinks. I soon found that *Sidral Mundet* (apple juice) was my standby. I had bought a jar of Instant Tea with me as being easier to cope with than tea leaves, and once persuaded Mina to have a cup, boiling the water up for her in a saucepan; however, she did not think much of it compared to her hot strong chocolate.

Mina's two little boys, small sturdy figures with jet black hair and enormous black eyes, soon accepted me as part of the household. Luis would greet me with a delighted and laborious '*Good* morn-ing' whenever I appeared, and spent a great many hours trying to persuade the parrot to make something of it too.

Margarita and I had soon got into the habit of having breakfast together in her room, and those morning discussions over our respective trays became something we both looked forward to. Usually we had papaya and limes, and sometimes an egg but I was always at a loss to know what to do with mine, since there were no egg cups in the house, as they are rarely used in Mexico.

'I always *meant* to buy one for a novelty!' exclaimed Margarita, breaking her egg neatly into a cup and adding butter, salt and pepper.

Sometimes on Sundays the pattern of the morning changed.

There would be no breakfast trays; instead Margarita and I would meet on the flower-shadowed patio in bathing costumes and go across the lawn to the swimming pool which lay glistening in the sun. Afterwards we would make our way leisurely back to the house to change, then go across the garden to Marta's house where the breakfast table would be laid with dishes of steaming *tamales*, the banana leaves in which they had been cooked, burning your fingers as you unwrapped the little packets. It always reminded me of a lucky dip for you never knew till you opened it whether the maize would be savoury and *picante*, or pale pink and tasting of strawberry. To follow there would be a large dish of the fluffy sweet pastry from the *panificadora* in San Angel, and pottery mugs of dark bitter chocolate flavoured with cinnamon.

Every time I was with Marta I remembered what had happened when the Russian Ballet visited Mexico City, and Margarita had taken her to see Irina Boronova dancing as the Doll in Petruchka at Bellas Artes.

'Martita was then three years old,' Margarita had told me, 'and afterwards we went backstage. She was ecstatic! Irina Boronova was taking off her make-up in her dressing-room and she looked down at Martita and said, "Would you like to be like me then?" Martita nodded, speechless. Irina tapped her lightly on the head. "Then you are!" she declared. Immediately, to our surprise, Martita began to dance round the dressing-room, then down the corridors and into the street. We had a five-seater car then and she kept dancing inside the car all the way home, and again when we were in the house. I could hardly get her to bed and she was up in the morning at six o'clock, dancing in her room and then in the garden. She hardly stopped all day even to eat, but went on dancing desperately. This went on for a day and a half, and I thought I must call the doctor for I saw her completely exhausted, yet she would not stop. Then suddenly I had an idea! "Come I will unwind you again, Martita!" I exclaimed, and I pretended to unwind the doll. She just collapsed then, and slept for a whole day!'

Often we would spend Sunday morning by the pool, all the family gathering there. Pepe, Marta's husband, who was a doctor, would revel in relaxing there after a hard week operating at the hospital. Sometimes a friend of his, a dentist, would join us. Both he and Pepe were experimenting with hypnosis instead of anaesthetic for operations so there would be long and interesting discussions for and against this as we lay on the grass in the sunshine. Finally, one or other of us, getting too hot, would dive into the pool again, to be followed in turn by everyone else.

Lunch would be one of Mina's special rice dishes in a huge brown *cazuela* flanked by *tortillas*, brought out by Antonio clad in a white jacket for the occasion. Sometimes we would have it in the dining-room, but it was always cold in there because these old Spanish houses with their wide patios were built with thick stone walls for the express purpose of keeping out the summer heat; because of this many of them now have central heating for the colder nights.

Friends of Margarita's—writers, artists or actors—would often be invited for coffee afterwards and we would have it sitting under a bower of mauve bougainvillea. An invitation to after-lunch coffee in Mexico means anything from four to five o'clock in the evening, in fact the question of when to arrive if you are invited for a meal is something quite on its own. If you are asked for seven o'clock dinner at night you are not expected to arrive before eight-thirty or nine, and dinner is quite likely to be served at ten; your hostess knows this and imagines that you do too. 'Lunch for one-thirty' means arriving at two-thirty. Before I realized this I once embarrassed a kind Mexican hostess by arriving at twenty-five past one, thinking it more polite than arriving just on the dot. She had to sit for an hour making polite conversation to me before the servant came in to announce that lunch was served! However, she forgave me because she knew that, being English, I had strange ideas about time. I soon learned to ask—half jokingly, but actually in all seriousness—'Mexican time or English time?' That saved me a lot of future embarrassment.

What I enjoyed about Margarita's entertaining was that much

of it was done in the garden. Huge yellow and black butterflies as large as bats sometimes flitted back and forth, and there were all sorts of birds. My favourite was the cardinal with his vivid red head and throat and black back—exactly like a cardinal, only more vivacious. 'Our first-class bird!' as Margarita called him affectionately. Occasionally there would be a humming bird, looking like a large dragonfly as it hovered with fast vibrating wings almost inside the cup of a flower.

There are almost a thousand different kinds of birds in Mexico. One bird-watching expedition totalled nearly three hundred different kinds in two weeks, some among the world's rarest species. Most of the more exotic ones are found in the coastal rain forests—the keel-billed toucan with his banana-like bill; the yellow-cheeked or red-crowned parrots which feed in the tops of the trees; the brilliantly coloured trogons—red, yellow and iridescent green all at the same time.

CHAPTER 4

GUADALUPE AND TEOTIHUACAN

T HE PYRAMID of Cuicuilco had created in me a feeling
of extraordinary anticipation, of wanting to 'go on from
there', so when I saw outside a small travel agency the
announcement, 'Tomorrow. Tour of Teotihuacán and the Pyramids,' I went in.

'They will leave at nine in the morning, señorita,' said the man,
handing me my ticket.

I arrived punctually at nine. Yes, the coach would be here any
minute. Ten past nine, twenty past. . . . '*Un momentito, señorita*'—
the proprietor pressed his thumb and first finger together delicately in a gesture one sees all over Mexico. The *momentitos*
mounted up. Half an hour passed, then the telephone rang. He
shrugged his shoulders apologetically.

'Alas, señorita, there has been a mistake. The bus, she is gone
somewhere else! But I shall not have you disappointed. I have
un primo (a cousin); if he is at home today he shall take you to the
Pyramids. He has a car; he is speaking good English.'

'But,' I began, 'supposing he doesn't . . .', but he was already
dialling the number.

'*Bueno? Quien Es?* Ah, Carlos . . .' and he launched into an
impassioned explanation. '*Si, si* . . .', in tones of deep satisfaction,
then to me, triumphantly, with the familiar gesture again, '*Un
momentito, señorita.*'

This time it was actually only ten *momentitos* before a car drew
up outside and in came *mi primo*, all smiles.

Carlos was a typical Mexican—dark-eyed, dark-haired, of
medium height and stocky build, and with a little toothbrush

moustache. He embraced his cousin and made me a little formal bow.

'You wish to see our Pyramids, señorita? I am happy to be of service.'

His cousin, cleared of all responsibility, came to the door and waved us off jovially.

On the outskirts of the city we came to the courtyard of a massive domed church. A throng of people was moving in and out and there were flashes of colour and faint sounds of music.

Carlos stopped the car. 'It is the Basilica of Guadalupe and today is fiesta. Do you like to go and see?'

On a platform in the shadow of the Basilica a small group of musicians was seated on straw-plaited chairs, while a group of Indian dancers in bright costumes stamped and whirled in a ritual dance. Their bare feet made no noise; the only sound was the high fluty music and the swishing of capes. The audience of shawled women, Indians with wide straw hats, their *zarapes* folded over their shoulders, young girls in summer dresses, and young men in open-necked shirts and new white hats were packed round the platform, intent and silent.

Beneath their gaudy head-dresses the shining, perspiring faces of the dancers were stern or expressionless; there was almost an air of desperation in the way they danced. A tiny boy, dressed in an identical miniature costume, was dancing as seriously and even more desperately than his elders, since, for all his fervour, his small legs could scarcely keep up with theirs. I had the feeling that they were dancing 'to' not 'for' someone, that had the audience melted away it would have made not the slightest difference. It was a strange spectacle to see inside the courtyard of a church.

'You see, when the Spaniards conquered Mexico,' explained Carlos, 'they put up a Christian Church everywhere they found an Indian temple. But they allowed the Indians to go on doing their dances outside—only they must now dance for the Holy Virgin. But often the Indians had only added the Holy Virgin to their own list of gods, so they were quite happy to dance for her as well!'

All over the courtyard little groups sat around on the ground surrounded by bundles and baskets. Some had brought their charcoal *braseros* and were roasting maize cobs or making *tortillas*, while mothers were feeding their babies oblivious to the passers-by. Meanwhile the crowds continued to pour into the courtyard, though not all were entering in the normal way. Many were advancing on their knees in an awkward shuffling movement.

'They are making a pilgrimage to ask some favour from the Virgin,' explained Carlos. 'Often their knees are bleeding before they reach the Altar. Many camp here for a week since their villages are miles away. Mexican Catholics think of Guadalupe as Europeans think of Lourdes.'

'Why?' I asked.

'Because in 1531, a poor Indian, Juan Diego, who had been converted by the priests, saw a beautiful Lady here who told him she was the Mother of God, and that he must go to the Bishop and tell him she wanted a church built here. The Bishop would not believe him, so at last she told him to climb to the top of that hill and gather flowers he would find there. Juan knew the hill was rocky and had no flowers, but he went, and on the bare rock he found roses. Very happy he gathered them into his *tilma*—his woven mantle—and took them to the Bishop. But more astonishing to the Bishop than the shower of roses that fell on his floor was that, on the inside of the *tilma*, was a beautiful image of the Holy Virgin, as if it was painted there!'

'What happened to the *tilma*?' I asked.

'It is inside. I will show it to you.'

Even coming in from the brilliant sunshine outside, the Basilica was a glittering spectacle with its silver decorations, the gold mosaic of the roof, and the great chandelier from which hundreds of cut-glass drops hung down like pearls. Kneeling figures were edging their way inch by inch up the aisles on the last stages of their painful pilgrimage.

Above the High Altar, in a frame of gold, silver and bronze, hung the *tilma* of Juan Diego. It showed the Virgin in a rose-coloured robe, her greenish blue mantle covered with eight-pointed gold stars. The *tilma*, about six feet long, was of coarse cloth woven from *maguey* fibres. Experts who have examined the Image are at a loss to understand how it was painted there or in what medium, or why, over four hundred years, during a hundred and sixteen of which it was not even under glass, it should not have faded.

Flowers, several feet deep, mostly gladioli and arum lilies, covered the steps of the altar and the floor. I remember especially the hollowed-out trunk of a banana tree filled with white gardenias, their scent intoxicating even in that incense-laden atmosphere.

'They have been carried on foot all the way from the little town of Fortin de las Flores in the State of Veracruz,' said Carlos.

In a side chapel were four glass coffins, three holding saints sent from Rome as skeletons covered in wax; in the fourth was a heavy bronze crucifix, badly twisted and lying on a silken cushion.

'That is what saved the *tilma* from being destroyed,' said Carlos. 'In 1921 someone put a stick of dynamite inside a bunch of flowers on the altar. Windows were broken and this crucifix, which was underneath the *tilma*, was thrown on the floor. But it saved the Image—even the glass frame was not broken. That is why it has been given this place of honour.'

A stream of pilgrims passed continually through this chapel, stopping to rub their hands reverently over the glass of each coffin, and then over themselves. A woman carrying a baby in her *rebozo* would unwrap it and rub her hands over its head and face; one held up the queue for quite five minutes because she had four small children, as well as a baby, each one of whom had to have a separate 'rub' from each coffin.

To Mexican Indians from the country their religion and their market are the most important things in life. Yet their lives were steeped in mysticism long before the Spaniards introduced them to Christianity, and I had the feeling that a pilgrimage such as this was the fulfilment of a need which went far deeper than they now understood.

One wall was hung from ceiling to floor with thousands of tiny silver tokens such as legs, arms, hearts, dogs, or pigs. Among them hung letters, bits of ribbon, scraps of hair (even whole pigtails), wedding sprays, photographs . . . all Thank Offerings or requests for favours.

'It must have taken generations to accumulate these!' I exclaimed.

Carlos shook his head. 'They come in hundreds! Every week they clean them all off and melt them down to make room for more. The wall plaques have been given by the wealthy people— that one is from a rich bullfighter . . . this one from an actress.'

We came out into brilliant sunlight again where the dancers were still whirling and stamping, and then we headed northwards. Because it was the Dry season the flat landscape was grey looking, relieved only by rows of the stiff dark-green *maguey* which grows everywhere on this Central Plateau. Some plants were as high as a man, their thick curved leaves with the serrated edges ending in a sharp point. Carlos stopped so that I could have a closer look.

'Once this plant provided everything the Indians needed,' he said, 'fibres for clothes, soap—even needle and thread! Look!' He tugged at the sharp thorny end and it came away with a long fibre attached to it. 'Now we only use it for *pulque*.'

He pointed to one huge plant from which the whole heart had been hacked out giving it a curiously desecrated appearance, and explained that *maguey* cannot be used for *pulque* until it is six years old, when it is ready to produce the one flower which is to be the climax of its existence. This is the moment the owner of the *maguey* is waiting for; at once, with his long *machete* knife, he cuts down the great stem up which the sap is about to rise, and hacks out the heart of the plant, leaving a basin-like hollow which slowly fills with sap.

Twice a day he 'milks' the plant of this *agua miel*, or honey water, sucking it up through a tube into a pigskin container—so the *maguey* is sometimes known as the Green Cow of Mexico. This goes on for six months, after which the plant dies.

When it is fresh, *agua miel* is splendid for the digestion but it soon starts to ferment, turning to a cloudy white substance four per cent alcoholic. That is when Mexicans love it, and there would probably be factories all over Mexico bottling this *pulque*, but for the fact that nobody has yet discovered how to make the corks stay on—since once it starts fermenting nobody can stop it. Served in special *pulquerias* in the cities, and the chief beverage of the farm workers, it is the poor man's beer.

Mexico is the only country in which *pulque* is made and the Indian legend tells that a rat-like animal was seen scraping the *maguey* stem with its teeth, retiring for a short time, then returning to drink the juice which had accumulated. The Indians copied its example to such good effect that in due course the Aztecs had a Goddess of *Pulque*. (As she had four hundred Rabbit Children drunkenness was measured in terms of rabbits—ten rabbits and you were slightly gay; forty rabbits and you had drunk enough to warrant being stoned to death; four hundred rabbits and you had drunk yourself to death.)

Houses were square boxes of *adobe* (clay mixed with grass to hold it together, then moulded into slabs and dried in the sun). Because they were the same colour as the earth the villages seemed to melt back into the landscape. Occasionally a house had been washed with lime, but usually this had flaked off, exposing the grey *adobe* underneath.

'It makes wonderful houses,' said Carlos, 'cool in summer and warm in winter. As long as you keep it well plastered with mud it will last for a hundred years. If you don't, it will just go back to mud when the rains come!'

(I had a vision of sitting in an *adobe* house in the rainy season while it melted away around me brick by brick.)

'But why no windows?' I asked. 'It must be so dark inside.'

'Windows cost money if you have glass. If you don't they let in the rain, and in the summer they let in too much heat.'

We drove on for an hour or more between fields of *maguey*,

then suddenly Carlos pointed to the left. I saw a brown truncated pyramid etched like a steel engraving against the blue. It was the Pyramid of the Sun, the focal point of the once mighty Ceremonial Centre of Teotihuacán.

As we walked across it appeared to fill the whole sky, its five tiers rearing upwards like gigantic steps.

No one knows for sure how high this Pyramid of the Sun was originally, since no one knows how high the temple was that stood on the top. Some people believe it to have been larger than Cheops in Egypt, but it is difficult to make comparison with the Egyptian pyramids since they all come to a point whereas the pyramids of Mexico are truncated, ending in a platform designed to hold a temple.

We made our way round the Pyramid and came out beside the great stairway which divided into two for a while then united again into a single ribbon to finish its dizzy ascent of two hundred and ten feet into the sky. It must have been a fantastic sight when the whole structure, covered in its original red painted stucco, glittered in sunlight on the floor of the gold dry valley. I took a deep breath and began the steep climb.

'Most of our pyramids were built over a hill to make a beginning,' said Carlos as we paused for breath, 'yet this one—one of our largest—is all artificial. The archeologists bored two tunnels through the base, from north to south and from east to west, to find out what was inside. It was full of *adobe* bricks made from the old rubbish beds of some people who must have inhabited this valley even earlier.'

As we continued climbing he dropped behind for a moment to examine some of the stucco more closely and so it happened that I was the first to reach the top. As I came level with it a yellow butterfly flittered across, so that for a moment there was just a pyramid meeting the sky and a butterfly hovering between them. (Into my mind flashed W. H. Davies—'A rainbow and a cuckoo's song may never come together again. May never come this side the tomb.' I held the thought and the moment in consciousness for the fraction of a second, but long enough to capture it. A butterfly

and a pyramid were not likely to come together again for me—
at any rate not this side of the tomb.)

From the platform which had once held the Temple to the
Sun God, I could see the Valley of Teotihuacán—'The Place
where all come to worship the Gods'—stretching away on all
sides. The silence was tremendous. It was as if it held within itself
the essence of all that had been etched upon the ethers of the
valley.

'Fresh archeological discoveries are being made every day in
Mexico,' said Carlos. 'You can find yourself many civilizations
behind in one night! For years we were taught that Teotihaucán
had been built by the Toltecs—that it was their great capital of
Tollan. Suddenly excavations at Tula gave absolute proof that
that was Tollan. So what everybody wants to know now is *who*
built Teotihuacán? It was already in ruins when the Aztecs
arrived in the Valley of Mexico. So now we just call them the
Teotihuacanos!'

We climbed down the great stairway again and walked the
length of the main axis of the Centre, nothing now but a rough
field track, though once it was lined with palaces and priestly
houses. Under each of the small grass-covered mounds that
reared up alongside at intervals there lay the crumbled remains
of some small truncated pyramid which, like an outstretched
palm, had once held a temple. The Spaniards, thinking they contained tombs, had christened this The Avenue of the Dead.

It is now known that there came a moment in the history of the
Teotihuacanos when they suddenly decided to completely re-
build their great Ceremonial Centre, apparently just at its peak of
perfection. They covered up the Pyramid of the Sun with twenty
feet of extra stucco, and in the case of other buildings half de-
molished the original then filled up the space with rubble to make
a solid base for another. The archeologists, in excavating such a
double building, just cut through the top one, remove the
débris that had been put in as a 'filler up', and there underneath is
the original building complete up to the line of demolition. What
seemed like the cellars of one building were really the bottom

half of the original house. It was strongly propped up with steel girders but all round the walls were remnants of fine murals in the original vivid red, mustard yellow and green. The plaster on which they had been painted was smooth and cold to touch.

Further on was the Citadel, an area inside a low rampart; round it were spaced isolated flat-topped pyramids. In the centre stood a raised altar with a flight of steps on each of its four sides.

'Thirteen in each flight,' pointed out Carlos, 'fifty-two altogether. Because of that some think this was one of the places where the Ceremony of the New Fire was held every fifty-two years.'

(Fifty-two years was the cycle at the end of which it was feared that the sun might not survive to sustain the world for another cycle. The Aztecs, for instance, believed that the world had already gone through five Suns, or Ages. The first one had been the Water Sun when the Supreme Being, whom they called Tloque Nahuaque, 'He from whom all come', first created the world; this Sun, they said, had been terminated by floods and lightning. Our present era they called the Sun of Fire. Each fifty-two year cycle was celebrated with great solemnity. The old altar fire which had burned perpetually for fifty-two years was extinguished, also all fires in the homes, and all pottery was smashed. The people spent the night with their priests in a Ceremonial Centre waiting anxiously to see if a certain star would reach the zenith—the signal that life would continue for another fifty-two years.)

'There is another reason why this might have been a site for the New Fire,' said Carlos. 'Do you see how the centre of this enclosure is in line not only with the top of the Pyramid of the Sun where we were just now, but also with the peak of that notched hill behind it? That must have some deep meaning because on that hilltop are more ruins. If the New Fire was lit here it would be seen from that hilltop. There the priests would light another which would be seen all over this valley.'

Once the Fire was rekindled swift runners bore it by torch to the temples where the people came to carry it to their homes.

New pottery was made; life commenced for another fifty-two years.

Behind the altar lay the Temple of Quetzalcoatl, God of Civilization, Learning and Culture, sometimes reported to have been blond and blue-eyed and to have come from across the sea. His cult, by contrast to that of many, was an ethical one of Brotherhood; it forbade human sacrifice and advocated instead the offering of birds, butterflies and flowers. He was also known as God of the Wind, as Venus the Morning Star and as the Plumed Serpent. It is because this temple at Teotihuacán has so many representations of a plumed serpent that it is known as the Temple of Quetzalcoatl. Small stone serpents, exquisitely carved, undulated sinuously round the walls, or emerged head-first out of it surrounded by a frill of feathers, while gigantic ones, into whose open fangs I could fit my whole hand, guarded the ramp of the stairway.

In a little Museum on the site lay the implements—chisels, polishers, grinders—which had been used to build and carve these pyramids and temples of Teotihuacán without the use of metal, simply by the cutting of stone upon stone. Sometimes they had used obsidan, or volcanic glass, chipping off red-hot razor-sharp flakes, but this was a brittle substance and hard to work with.

There were also figurines which had been found inside the Pyramid of the Sun, the earlier ones crude, later ones hand-moulded into such perfect features that they might have been portraits. Here had been a highly civilized community—so skilled in architecture and astronomy that when they built that colossal Pyramid of the Sun they orientated its great mass with such delicate precision that it faced the setting sun on the day it crossed the zenith; so advanced in agriculture that they were already cultivating (as well as maize, beans, chile and tomatoes) a great many plants not then known to the Old World, while the cotton they spun varied from the fineness of silk to the thickness of velvet.

Nobody knows what could have happened to cut down the

flower of such a civilization in the fullness of perfection. One theory is that the sudden large-scale reconstruction of the whole city, with perhaps the changeover to some new god, may have upset the masses and caused a revolt. Again, since the whole zone was paved with lime cement and the walls of buildings covered with it this meant that the Teotihuacanos made quantities of charcoal in order to reduce the limestone, and this may have led to the denuding of surrounding forests, followed by soil erosion and the failure of the crops. Whatever it was, the fall of Teotihuacán, as well as its origin, still remains a mystery.

This period, from A.D. 200 to 900 (the so-called Classic Period), was one of the greatest in the history of Mexico and Central America. Whilst the Teotihuacanos were constructing this mighty metropolis here, deep in the jungle State of Veracruz—where the Olmecs had already carved the great basalt heads of their gods— the Totonacs were worshipping at the superb seven-storey Pyramid of El Tajín; southwards in Oaxaca the Zapotec culture was at its height in the great Ceremonial City of Monte Albán; further south still, the Old Mayan Empire, which already had a calendric and counting system equal, if not superior, to that of the Romans, was reaching the heady peak of fulfilment with the magnificent pyramids and palaces of Palenque, Copán and Tikal.

Meantime, on the other side of the world, the Jutes, the Angles and the Saxons were just setting out across the North Sea in open boats to establish a kingdom on the island of Britain. Long before Canute became King of England the mighty civilization of Teotihuacán had already passed into oblivion.

CHAPTER 5

THE MURALS OF DIEGO RIVERA

ONE OF THE HIGHLIGHTS for me was the day I discovered the murals of Diego Rivera in the National Palace. I marvelled then that I had passed its rather severe façade so many times without having some premonition of what lay within.

The Palace also contains the Archives, the National Treasury and other Government departments, and I had wandered in there that day amidst a coming and going of Government workers and found myself in the main courtyard. With its colonnades of grey stone it was gloomy even in the strong sunlight, but as I started to climb the huge stairway, which divided into two sweeping curves, I had that sudden sensation of being steeped in colour that comes with walking in high summer between two lavish herbaceous borders, for the walls of the staircase were a glowing panorama of face and form almost bewildering in intensity and colouring and this tableau of colour continued to unfold itself round the gallery overlooking the dingy courtyard.

These were the murals of Diego Rivera, Mexico's leading muralist—or rather, *some* of them, for they adorn almost every important public building in Mexico City. I saw many others later but, for me, these in the National Palace remained startling . . . beautiful . . . the best . . . their detail so perfect that I felt I could never reach the end of discovery.

They depict the whole history of Mexico from the days of the Aztecs and the arrival of the Spaniards, to the subsequent Revolutionary struggles for Independence.

Having already, through the impact of the Pedregal, been

drawn into that aura of archaic civilization which still trembles around Cuicuilco, and then touched the fringe of the vanished greatness of Teotihuacán, it seemed somehow perfectly natural to find myself looking at the next step in the tempestuous life-story of Mexico—the glittering glory that had been Tenochtitlan, the mighty Empire of the Aztecs.

The mural showed a city of islands laid out in geometrical perfection, covered in shining houses and temples, intersected by glittering canals, and joined to the mainland by magnificent causeways. Everything led the gaze inwards to a gigantic central court of pyramids, in the centre of which, sumptuous and splendid, rose the Great Teocali, the twin-towered Pyramid, dedicated to the gods of War and of Rain, the two most important events in the life of the Aztecs. In the background, a landmark then as now for every traveller in the Valley of Mexico, rose Popocatépetl and Ixtaccíhuatl.

Even through its medium of paint the shining scene cast such a spell over the drab courtyard that I could well understand that when the Spaniards first glimpsed the reality in the full splendour of sunlight they thought it a city built of silver, so that their historian, Bernal Díaz del Castillo, wrote, 'Gazing on such wonderful sights we did not know what to say, or whether what appeared before us was real!'

The Aztec legend tells that about A.D. 1160, when they were only a wandering tribe of nomads, their High Priest Tenoch was told by their tribal god, Mexictli, to lead them forth until he saw an eagle sitting on a cactus eating a serpent, and there to establish his dynasty.

For over two hundred years the little tribe wandered until, in 1325, in the centre of the great lake Texcoco, Tenoch saw a small muddy island. On it an eagle was perched on a green *nopal* cactus with a serpent in its mouth. Upon that island the Aztecs founded their city under their first king Acamapictli—Bunch of Cane Stalks. They called the city Tenochtitlan after their leader Tenoch and the Aztec word *titlan*, meaning 'a cactus growing under a rock'. Because their tribal god was Mexictli the people became known as Mexica and their country Mexico (in Aztec the ending 'a' signifies a people and 'o' a place). Today, an eagle sitting on a cactus with a serpent in his mouth appears not only on the national flag of Mexico and the coat of arms but also on the coinage.

The islands of Tenochtitlan had been formed by building huge rafts, covering them with soil and saplings, and anchoring them round the original island until, with time, roots and silt sank down to the shallow lake bed, forming individual islands. Since there were no wheeled vehicles and no beasts of burden everything was carried by runners, or in flat-bottomed boats on the intersecting canals.

As in Teotihuacán mighty serpent heads flanked the great stairway of the main Temple. That centre courtyard held over seventy-two buildings as well as fountains and gardens. One of its less pleasant structures, the Altar of Skulls, consisted of real skulls threaded on poles embedded in mortar. These were the victims of innumerable human sacrifices, for the Aztecs went in for this on a tremendous scale, tearing out the still-beating hearts and offering them up to the War god. Yet it was not done through wanton cruelty but from a passionate desire for the preservation of the community, for they believed that the gods had moulded man from dough, moistened with their own blood. Because it contained the blood of the gods it came to life. Then the gods departed to the sky to become the Sun, the Moon and the other elements in order to make the earth fertile.

For the Sun to fight the army of stars every night he needed to be fed continually with the precious life-giving substance the gods had given to man—human blood. Hence it was the job of man on earth to serve the gods and feed them on human hearts—for if they died, who were the powers of nature, all humanity must die with them. It was a vicious circle if ever there was one, but it explains the necessity for human sacrifice, which lasted longer in Mexico than in most places. The Aztecs, thinking to make their gods even more powerful, increased the number of their sacrifices to terrible proportions and it was the constant necessity of finding enough victims which caused them to make so many wars and raids upon their neighbours and eventually made them hated throughout the Valley of Mexico. In the end this led to their downfall for it made the other tribes ally themselves with the Spaniards against them.

But in this mural Diego Rivera shows Tenochtitlan at the height of its glory. In the foreground was the market, brilliant and colourful, the Aztec officials, magnificent in feather cloaks, had their black hair swept up and secured by gold bands. Goods were being bartered for, not sold—beans for fish . . . *tortillas* for fruit . . . and the balance paid in *cacao* beans which were used as currency. A Totonac trader was paying his tribute to the Aztec rulers with a transparent feather quill filled with gold dust; an Aztec General was offering a human arm as a gift to a beautiful young woman, assuring her that, as it was the right arm of the sixth enemy he had captured for sacrifice, it was particularly valuable. (The face of the young woman is a portrait of Diego Rivera's wife, Frieda, whose face appears on countless murals. A talented painter herself, and bedridden for years after a car accident, she had a mirror fixed on her ceiling so that she could paint self-portraits from her bed.)

Behind the pottery sellers two black dogs, about the size of a fox terrier, were standing nose to nose. These were the Mexican hairless dogs whose bare black skin is so hot and dry that it is like touching hot rice paper—they have a metabolism of 104 degrees.

In Argentina the Indians used to take them to bed as a cure for rheumatism and colds (being hairless, they are also flealess); but in Mexico they were sometimes fattened up on maize and eaten as a ritual meal, for they had a special spiritual significance to the Aztecs. Their official name was Xoloizcuntle (shoolo-is-cuint-li)—'The earthly representative of the god Xolotl'—he whose duty it was to escort the newly-dead to their correct destination. Hundreds of ancient tombs in Mexico have been found to contain a clay model of a smooth plump dog with pricked-up ears and a laughing expression. He was there to carry his charge across the wide river which he would have to cross during his difficult journey on the other side of death. The spirit of the deceased also had to negotiate eight deserts and endure many other hardships before he finally reached the place for which he had fitted himself in one of the Nine Regions of the Land of the Dead. Persons dying in battle, by sacrifice, through drowning or in childbirth went directly to a special heaven. Above all these lay the various heavens in which the gods dwelt according to their rank in the Hierarchy, the Original Creator living in the topmost one.

(I found that if I looked long enough a hairless dog was to be found on almost every one of the murals. In the same way I found the signature of Diego Rivera several times: on a round pot, on the blade of a *machete* knife, and near the bare foot of a branded Indian.)

The whole life of the Aztec was dedicated to keeping the gods happy—and since there was one for each day of his 260-day Ritual Calendar this was a full-time occupation. The names of some of them were fascinating: He from the Sea Snail; God of Straw and Numbers; Obsidian Knife Butterfly; Goddess of Salt and of the Dissolute; He who makes Things Sprout. Some of their Ritual Ceremonies were less fascinating—the drowning of a boy and girl in a canoe filled with human hearts; dances by priests wearing human skins; men and children beating women with straw-filled bags to make them cry to bring rain . . .

Other murals showed the arrival of Cortés with his tiny army of several hundred men and sixteen horses; the latter were a new phenomena to the Aztecs who at first imagined horse and rider to be a single unit. The story of the Spanish Conquest has been told many times, and never better than by Prescott in his *Conquest of Mexico*, so sufficient to say that though the Spaniards were treated royally as half-guest and half-god when they first reached Tenochtitlan (because of the legend that Quetzalcoatl would return one day as a bearded blond man), the Aztecs were soon left in no doubt as to their real intentions—conquest, and gold for Spain.

A terrible massacre of the Indians took place at Cholula; Aztecs in Tenochtitlan were attacked and killed by the Spaniards while they were celebrating one of their feast days; finally the Aztec Emperor, Moctezuma, was stoned to death by his own people on his palace roof because he would not take a firm stand and turn Cortés out of the city. The Spaniards were forced to retreat with the Aztecs attacking them from all sides by land and water. Weighed down with stolen gold they suffered terrible losses, many of them drowning with their treasures in the canals.

But now, though the Spaniards had been driven out of the city, a new terror overtook the Aztecs. A negro slave who had accompanied the Spaniards had smallpox. The Spaniards were immune to it but it was a completely new disease in America, and it swept like fire through Tenochtitlan. The Aztecs died in thousands, while outside, Cortés, his depleted forces strengthened by an army of Indian allies who, like so many of the tribes in the Valley of Mexico, had a grudge against the Aztecs because of their endless raids for sacrificial victims, commenced a fresh assault. This time he razed the buildings to the ground as he went, and set fire to them.

The new Emperor, young Cuauhtémoc, nephew of the dead Moctezuma—whose statue was now such a familiar sight to me on Reforma—made a heroic stand against him during the terrible siege that lasted more than seventy days. Not till his people were so weakened by disease and starvation, the canals and causeways so deep in dead bodies that the survivors were walking upon them, did the young Emperor yield. By then the lovely shining city of Tenochtitlan was reduced to a heap of smoking ruins.

All this had taken place, not in some far-off part of the country but on the very spot on which I stood—for less than ten feet below the muddy foundations of the National Palace, the Cathedral and the *zocalo* of Mexico City lie the tragic ruins of Moctezuma's Palace and the great Temple Courts of Tenochtitlan.

With the fall of the Aztec Empire Cortés became the first Ruler of New Spain, as it was called; after him, during the three centuries of Spanish rule that followed, came sixty-one Viceroys.

Thousands of Spaniards came over and took up huge estates and the Indians became their slaves while the Spanish Inquisition kept order in the country. Many of the friars who accompanied the Spaniards, horrified at the way the Indians were treated, spent their lives trying to help them.

Yet, economically, there was much growth, for the Spaniards introduced new methods of farming, the use of the wheel, beasts of burden like the horse and the donkey and new items of diet such as wheat, sugar cane, pulses and apples.

The population soon became divided into three classes—the oppressed Indians; the *mestizos* (the result of intermarriage between Indians and Spaniards); and the *creoles* (of pure Spanish parentage, but born in New Spain) who had the important Government posts. At the very top were the few men from Spain for whose benefit the colony was run and who had the monopoly of all the Government jobs. Nobody thought of rebellion; if they did there was always the Inquisition.

In these murals Diego Rivera has painted all the contradictory threads that have gone to make up the pattern that is Mexico— the grace of the Indian women bent over their *metates* (grinding bowls) of volcanic stone, or slapping their *tortillas* from hand to hand; the lonely dignity of Indians planting out the maize with their digging sticks; the quiet composure of the children; the Indian's love for colour, not only in his *fiestas* but round his own *adobe* hut—these things are still to be seen all over Mexico.

Then he shows you the other side of the picture—the whips of the Spanish overseers in field and mine; the brandings, the hangings, the burnings and the executions of the Inquisition; the mounting poverty and misery of the masses, and finally, like a pent-up volcano—Revolution!

From the moment that he saw the Renaissance Frescoes in Europe he knew what he wanted to do for Mexico with his art, and he dedicated the whole of his life to it. I doubt if any country in the world has a record of its history in such colour, and with such faithful representation of features, as Diego Rivera has given to Mexico through his murals.

After this I came often to sit on the edge of the stone fountain outside the Cathedral. Five hundred years before I would have been sitting within the very precincts of the Temple Court of the Aztecs with the Great Tcocali looming up almost on top of me. On the other side of the road I could see, through the railings that protected them, all that remains of its foundations. They lay below pavement level, ignored for the most part by the passers-by . . . a few worn stone steps . . . a huge stone serpent's head . . . some scraps of paving. To find the rest would mean digging up the whole *zocalo*, demolishing the Cathedral, the National Palace, and most of the important buildings of the city centre, for almost anywhere you dig down under this part of the city you are liable to find sculptured treasures of stone, silver or gold.

In the courtyard of the National Museum round the corner was one of the greatest of these treasures—the great Calendar Stone of the Aztecs, the Stone of the Sun. Weighing about twenty-four tons this great engraved olivine basalt stone was discovered in 1790 under the *zocalo* by the Spaniards. Scientists and mathematicians all over the world have tried to unravel the secret contained within its nine decorative circles with their 1,878 symbols. In the centre is the Face of the Sun; the four squares surrounding it are believed to represent those four great Cosmic Ages, or Suns, through which the Aztecs believed the world had already passed.

The priests of those advanced early cultures had not only to forecast actual disasters for their community—such as floods and earthquakes—but also to maintain a perfect balance between the astral world and the earth world, so it meant that all their ritual ceremonies had to coincide exactly with astronomical events. Of necessity, therefore, they had an incredibly deep knowledge of astronomy, and already the great Arrow of Tonatiuh which appears on the Stone has been identified as having a calendar value of 2,920 days, equal to five synodical revolutions of Venus, or eight calendar years of 365 days each. The distinguished Mexican mathematician, Dr. Raoul Noriega, who has written a 445-page volume on the Stone, believes that its esoteric message, if correctly deciphered, may well throw new light, not only on our concept of time, but on man's whole relationship to the Universe.

'Yet you know,' said Margarita one day as we stood together studying the Stone, 'Dr. Alfonso Caso, our greatest archeologist, says that even this is nothing compared to what is still buried below the *zocalo*! When they were digging there they found an even greater Stone. It would have cost thousands of *pesos* to raise it so they covered it up again. When they dug up the *zocalo* last time to remove the trees, Dr. Caso asked, "Why not make the excavations *now*? It would soon pay for itself. Who wouldn't pay to go in tunnels to see those treasures that lie there?" But the Mayor wanted to get the *zocalo* finished in a hurry for a 16th September Parade and it was never done. So everything is still lying underneath our feet!'

On the other side of the *zocalo*, where Moctezuma's Palace had once stood, on the roof of which he was stoned to death, stood the National Pawnshop. Its galleries were stacked with everything from the chandeliers of the aristocracy to the iron bedsteads or cooking pots of the very poor. Families who have emigrated to the city from the country are quite used to sleeping on *petate* mats so that when they are hard-up the bedstead is often the first thing to go. A rather unusual feature is that Mexican craftsmen can display and sell their goods here only it must be at a special low price decided by experts in order to cut out the middle man and benefit the shopper. The street outside the Pawnshop is haunted by men known as *coyotes*, or wolves, who buy pawn tickets and sell them again for a few *pesos* more. Whether the Pawnshop is half empty or packed to capacity depends on what is going on in Mexico City. When Manolete, the famous Spanish matador, came to fight here it was packed out. Everybody wanted to go to the Bull Fight—and it was a hundred *pesos* that day for a seat in the sun. (In the ordinary way posters may read, 'Seats in the shade 32 *pesos*. In the sun 20 *pesos*. Women and children in the sun 10 *pesos*.')

Finding my way about the city was simplified for me once I

discovered that streets were grouped under 'species'; for instance you only needed to come across *Schumann* to know that you were on the right track for *Paganini*; or to stumble upon *Heliotrope* to know that before long you would run *Magnolia* to earth.

There were always street vendors selling Lottery tickets, profits from which are used for Public Health Projects. The new Medical Centre in Mexico City, the largest in Latin America, was paid for by the National Lottery. Three times a week twenty-four boys aged between eight and twelve, chosen for character and intelligence, and dressed as bellboys, draw the tickets in the auditorium of the Lottery Building. Forty thousand numbered wooden balls are tumbled over and over with a roar in a huge electrically-operated brass cage; the balls printed with the prizes are in a smaller hand-operated one. No adult employee of the Lottery is allowed to touch the balls once they are in the cages. Tickets cost from 7s. 6d. to £60 each according to the prize, which can be as much as £700,000. Poorer people usually buy a ticket between them—known as a *vaca* (a cow), because several people milk it, each one in the group being known as a *vaquero* (cowboy). Before the drawing is over the next batch of tickets is already being rolled off in the basement.

The Lottery Building, like the Latin America Tower, is earthquake proof. I sometimes took the lift up to the forty-fourth storey of the latter, the tallest building in the city, which has an observation platform with a spectacular view right out to the volcanoes. Though it is five hundred and ninety-seven feet high, and weighs twenty-five thousand tons, it was not even damaged by the last earthquake in June 1957 when more than a dozen large buildings were shattered.

The earthquake started at 2.35 a.m., and actually lasted less than one minute. 'The Long Minute!' exclaimed one Mexican who was talking to me about it. 'I felt a tremendous shake,' he added, 'then heard something like a big wind. The light had been cut—they always cut it at once because of fire—but suddenly I saw a corner of the room opening and closing, then little pieces began to fall. I grabbed my wife and pushed her into the doorway.

That's the place to stand! The walls may fall all round you and the arch may shake—but it seldom falls. After the first shake we ran out into the street. Telephone poles were swaying and high-tension wires were snapping and making sparks. There was a tremendous noise as one nine-storey building came down in a cloud of dust. It was brand new but poorly built—too much sand in the cement. The foundation is the main thing—once something snaps down there the walls just fall outwards like icing on a cake. The sort of earthquakes we get in Mexico City are oscillatory,' he added—'like rocking backwards and forwards in a hammock—not the quick up-and-down ones. Ours are caused by the earth settling and they don't really do much damage because Mexico City is built on water and mud—not rock like San Francisco!'

He explained that all the earthquake-proof buildings, like the Lottery Building and the Latin America Tower, are built on a special hydraulic foundation like a huge floating barge so that they just sway back and forth with the movement of the earth without even their windows breaking. These barge-like foundations also help to solve another problem of Mexico City which is that so much water has been drained from the lake bed on which it stands that the ground is always sinking, but not evenly, so that many of the older buildings, like the Basilica of Guadalupe, lean noticeably to one side. Sometimes you will come across an entrance that has acquired a couple of steps down in order to compensate for this sinking.

I could quite understand now why it is forbidden to put gas pipes underground in Mexico City; also why this is one of the largest cities in the world without an underground railway system. It would be geologically and technically impossible to put one there.

As to transportation, I had soon found that if ever you were in a hurry the best way of getting anywhere in the City was by *peso* taxi. These are ordinary taxis which periodically turn themselves into *peso* taxis by the simple process of the driver holding one finger out of the window as he drives along. This indicates that for one *peso* you may travel any distance between two fixed points, say the length of Insurgentes, or right down Reforma as far as the *zocalo*. To summon a *peso* taxi you simply stand on the kerb holding up one finger appealingly; Reforma and Insurgentes are a forest of such fingers in the morning rush-hour.

Five passengers can be fitted into a taxi in this way and once I overheard an animated conversation between two ladies who were having trouble with their domestic staff—the garden boy had had to be sacked that morning for slashing the house-boy across the face with a knife while under the influence of *tequila*. Violence of this sort is more prevalent on the Plateau than in other parts of Mexico, probably because of the effect of the high altitude on the nerves; even race horses arriving from lower altitudes have to be acclimatized.

CHAPTER 6

BENITO JUAREZ AND JESUS URUETA

ONE DAY I took a *peso* taxi back from Insurgentes. As the driver was going right on to San Angel he said he would drop me at the door.

'What is the name of the people?' he asked.

'It's the house of the writer Margarita Urueta,' I answered.

'Not the daughter of Jesús Urueta?' exclaimed the other occupant of the *peso* taxi, an elderly gentleman.

I nodded.

'I once heard him talk,' he said in a voice almost of reverence. 'It was amazing! I could have gone on listening for hours!'

'Margarita, do tell me something about your father,' I said that evening as we sat in the library after supper. 'There was a man in the *peso* taxi today who said he had heard him talk. He sounded so thrilled about it!'

Margarita pointed to the manuscript on which she had been working ever since my arrival on that January evening.

'I am making his biography now!' she replied. 'But to really understand why he made his speeches you have to know what was happening at that time in our country. It is not a too happy story! After three hundred years of being just a Spanish Colony Mexicans wanted their Independence. By then there were not only Spanish and Indians, but also the *mestizos*, a mixture of both. But the Spaniards had the Government positions and owned the big *haciendas* (estates). The *mestizos* were the tradesmen, and the pure Indians were just slaves on the *haciendas*.

'Everywhere in Mexico,' she went on, 'you will see "Hidalgo" as the name of a street. It was on 15th September 1810—and that date you will see too as a street name—that Father Miguel Hidalgo, who wanted to rescue the Indians from this terrible cruelty and oppression, made his great speech that we call *El Grito* (The Cry). It said, "We have no other choice than to go out and destroy the Spaniards!" The next day, 16th September—which is now our National Day of Independence, and the biggest holiday in Mexico—he and his small group of Revolutionaries started the War for Independence. But his inexperience in fighting made him lose the battle. One by one they were caught by the Spaniards and killed. Father Hidalgo was shot and his head cut off. A young priest, Father José Morelos (another great Mexican hero), took his place as leader. He was shot too. But at last, in 1821, after ten hard years of struggling, we got our Independence from Spain!

'But that was only the beginning of our struggle,' went on Margarita. 'One President after another came into power—altogether we had forty Presidents and two Emperors in that first hundred years of Independence. Some were only in office for a week or even a day! You will find streets all over Mexico named after Presidents—and others named after heroes who fought first against the Spaniards and then against the Presidents, because *they* were sometimes as domineering as the Spaniards had been.'

'Tell me about some of them,' I begged.

'Well, first we had General Augustine Iturbide. He called himself Emperor Augustin I of Mexico—but he only lasted ten months. He was exiled and afterwards shot. The worst one was Santa Anna. He was a cruel dictator for twenty-five years. But at last a man appeared who had what Mexico needed so badly—high ideals and vision. He also had great ambitions—but not for himself, only for his country. His name was Benito Juárez. He was a pure-blooded Zapotec Indian from Oaxaca—and he became our finest President. He was a lawyer and the Treasury of Oaxaca was bankrupt when he took over as Governor. When he left office—without a penny—he left fifty thousand *pesos* in the Treasury! He was so completely honest—and that was something rare in those days in the Government—and all through his life he kept this honesty. When he became President of Mexico he began to bring in his great Reform Laws—we call it the Constitution of 1857. It is still the basis for our present Constitution.'

Margarita went on to explain that what Juárez wanted to do was to free the country from the power of the Church and the Military, who owned most of the land and money. Most of the population were just slaves, working for them without any payment except food and clothing. They did not even own the huts they lived in. Juárez insisted that all Church property not actually being used as a place of worship must be sold. He did not want to confiscate it—the Church could have the money for it—but he wanted the land to be shared out among the Indians to whom it really belonged. Monasteries and convents were closed, education was secularized, the army was reduced, and freedom was given to the Press.

'This time it was a Government of intellectuals and idealists,' went on Margarita. 'No time in our history shows such great figures—and not one of them made a fortune through being in the Government. That was something quite unique in Mexico! It gives you a real idea of the character of the silent grave-faced Indian who was their leader. He is to Mexico what Lincoln is to the United States. On the hottest day he would be seen in his black suit driving in a small carriage along the dusty roads to visit all the little towns and villages. But first he had to fight his way through three terrible years of Civil War. And not only that. Encouraged by the Church and the big landowners, Napoleon III sent an army to try and set up a French Empire in Mexico. But all the people were behind Juárez, and he beat the French in a big battle at Puebla on the 5th May 1862.'

'So that is why I have seen Cinco de Mayo on the side of so many buses?' I exclaimed.

Margarita nodded. 'It is the name of a big street, and also a National Holiday. After the French were defeated the Church and the Conservatives, saying it was in the name of the Mexican people, invited the Archduke Maximilian of Austria, brother of Napoleon III, to become Emperor of Mexico. Thinking it was

the will of all the people he came with his wife Carlotta. She wept
when she saw what a cold reception they got when they landed
at Veracruz—it was only at the point of the French bayonets!'
'But they did stay?' I asked.

Margarita nodded. 'For three years we had the Emperor
Maximilian. He lived grandly in Chapultepec Castle. He gave
to Mexico much in the French style, such as its avenues. But all
the time the Mexican people were waiting, gathering round
Juárez in the hills. Step by step his forces reoccupied the main
towns. Then Napoleon withdrew the French Army, which was
the only thing that kept Maximilian on his throne. Juárez sent
out an order for his capture and execution but at the same time he
warned Maximilian to fly from the country while there was time.
Maximilian did not believe Juárez meant to hurt him and he
refused to go. He was a good man, but he was captured, and
Juárez said to him, "We *have* to kill you because we have to give
an example to the country that we mean to have a Republic."
Then Maximilian *did* try to escape. But it was too late—he had
had his chance. The Empress Carlotta fled to Europe and begged
Napoleon and the Pope to send an army to help her husband. She
was so unhappy that she went insane. (This has been the theme of
many Mexican playwrights.) Maximilian was shot with two of
his Generals on the Hill of Bells in Querétaro on the 19th June
1867.'

'What did Juárez do then?' I asked.

'Well, all this time he had never stopped fighting for the people,
trying to break up the big estates so that the land could be shared
out among them. But besides his big Reforms there was so much
to do. Presidents before him had piled up terrible national debts
with foreign countries. Mexico owed money to England . . . to
France . . . to Spain. . . Juárez set to work to pay all these debts
to restore the economy of the country. It was an immense task,
but he never hesitated. In 1871 he was re-elected as President for a
second time. Now it seemed that his dreams for Mexico would
come true at last. Then on 18th July 1872, suddenly—a heart
attack—and Juárez was dead!'

'Oh *no*!' I exclaimed involuntarily. I had been living the story with her . . . with Mexico. I could not bear that it should end like that.

'Now,' said Margarita, 'you will understand when I tell you of my father's speeches—for with all his heart and soul he upheld the ideals of Benito Juárez. But now there came as President a General, Porfirio Díaz. He had envied Juárez and he seized power without being elected. For thirty-four years he ruled as a dictator. He kept Mexico at peace—but only by force. Everything Juárez had tried to do was as nothing. All his great Reforms were pushed on one side. The new President and his friends in the Government built up great power and fortunes for themselves and for the ruling classes while millions of Indians went back to being just the slaves of the landowners.

'My father, at this time, was only a child. When he was born, in February 1867, Juárez was just winning the war against Maximilian. When my father was three years old my grandparents had to flee by coach from Chihuahua in the north because of attacks from the Indians. They came to live in Mexico City in a street that was then called *Plateros* because it had all the silver shops. Today it is called "Francisco I Madero".

'When he was older my father went as a student to the Law School, but already he had begun to attract the attention of everybody with his speeches as an exponent of Greek history. Then he went to Europe to study law, and in Paris he became a friend of Rodin. He gave my father the original plaster cast of his head of Victor Hugo. My sister Cordelia has it now in her studio.

'It was in France that my father first learned of the Liberal Movement,' continued Margarita. 'It filled him with hope, for he could see that it held the only possibility for Mexico—which was for Mexicans to be just *Mexicans* instead of this conflicting mixture of Spanish, Indians and *mestizos*. In 1903 he was sent back to Paris to represent Mexico at the Convention of Historians. He had just married—that was his honeymoon too!

'On his return from Paris he found a new Revolution germinating in Mexico. The whole country was sick to death of the dictatorship of Porfirio Díaz. It is true he had made plenty of industries—but only to get power for himself and his friends. Everything in the country was mortgaged to foreign investors— and the poor were poorer than ever. And that was when my father began his political speeches for Liberalism!' ended Margarita.

It was long past midnight by the time we went up to bed, and during the days that followed my thoughts were full of what Margarita had told me—of Benito Juárez . . . of Jesús Urueta. As is often the case when something awakens a response in you it seems to set up a chain reaction, for almost immediately, I was invited to tea by Cordelia, Margarita's sister, one of the leading women artists of Mexico. An exhibition of her paintings was soon to be held at Bellas Artes and she was busy sorting out the can- vasses. They were huge surrealist works, vivid and beautiful— challenging both to the eye and the mind. After tea she placed them one after the other against the wall for me to see, turning them first one way and then another. I was fascinated by the change of mood and imagery they conjured up for me according to which way up you looked at them.

Just as I was leaving I caught sight of a white bust on the mantelshelf.

'Is *that* the plaster cast of Victor Hugo that Rodin gave your father?' I asked.

Cordelia nodded. She picked it up and handed it to me. Under- neath I noticed little criss-cross pieces of wood covering a tin lid which had been put in to block up the hole in the base.

'That paintpot lid was fixed there by Rodin,' said Cordelia. 'I stuck these strips of wood across to keep it safe! It is the ori- ginal cast of the head which the Germans stole from Paris during the last war. My father always kept it in his library.'

Shortly after this I met the Mexican writer from Chihuahua, Martina Barrios Alvarez.

'So you are staying with Margarita Urueta!' he exclaimed. 'You know, of course, that her father, Jesús Urueta, was the greatest orator Mexico has ever had! He was also the one who had the greatest Hellenic culture in Latin America at that time—

he could speak on the Greek history as no one had ever done. Many people who used to love him changed that for hatred when he became a Revolutionary—but it was because he had realized that his words were not only for the recreation of souls but also an instrument at the service of the people, to wake up the conscience where the dictatorship of Porfirio Díaz had kept the Mexicans down.

'He was born in my town of Chihuahua,' he went on, 'and came there several times to speak when he was an eminent Tribune. Once he had to attend a big birthday celebration there of one of our Governors. Of course, he was expected to give a speech, but half-way through the lunch he felt ill and had to be taken home. When they arrived there he recovered instantly. "You see, I never felt better in my life," he told the friend who had taken him home. "But I cannot talk at the birthday of a General who has become a Conservative! I belong to the Liberal Party!" Afterwards he went back and made a brilliant speech for Juárez and the Liberals!

'Another time he came to Chihuahua on the Centenary of Juárez to give a big conference in the Theatre of the Heroes. All Chihuahua was there to hear him! Oh, if you could have seen him when he was talking—he was like an illuminated man!' Señor Alvarez's eyes glowed with enthusiasm. 'Yet he was so tremendously modest. He would sit all curled up before the speeches, as if he could not say a word. But as soon as he advanced on to the platform he would become so tall and important you could hardly believe it. He would look at the whole aspect of the theatre, then, with his words, his hands, and those magnetic eyes of his, he so hypnotized his audience that you could have heard a pin drop! When he had finished he was exhausted!'

'Oh, how I *wish* I could have heard him!' I exclaimed fervently.

'Well, I can tell you some parts of that speech he made in Chihuahua for I know much of it by heart!' and Señor Alvarez began to quote phrases full of fire and fervour, of poetry and tenderness; phrases, like this that have remained with me ever since—

'. . . and Benito Juárez, his hands knotted behind upon his

[64]

coat-tails, walked slowly down the silent street with a dawn in his soul . . .'

'I can tell you exactly how he finished that speech,' went on Señor Alvarez. 'He ended it like this: "And if one day—let us hope to God it doesn't happen—our nationality is again in danger, and we are again the victims of fraud and aggression, then, in the graveyard of our history, the Tables of the Law will fall down from the knees of Juárez, warning that it is time to save the country again, and the great man will be awakened from his sleep and will come again amongst us. And oh, feeling him at our side, even though steel hands may hold our bodies, we shall have, like him, our spirit filled with hope, and our eyes fixed upon the stars!" '

When he finished there was a deep silence. It was he who finally broke it.

'You know,' he said, 'a Mexican writer once said, "If anyone is speaking of eloquence in Mexico, he is speaking of Jesús Urueta. Not of the coward word of one who adulates himself, but of the word of a man used as an instrument . . . a song . . . a thought . . . as a sound that comes directly to the spirit." This, he says, is enough for Jesús Urueta to be eventually in the graveyard of the Immortals. I think there is nothing I can add to that!' finished Señor Alvarez.

'Margarita, *please* go on telling me about your father,' I begged next day. 'What happened to him afterwards? And how *did* Mexico get a change of Government from Porfirio Díaz?'

'Well,' said Margarita, 'the last question first! At that time there was one man who gave us hope. His name was Francisco I Madero, and though he was a rich landowner, he was well known for his kindness to the *peóns* (peasants) who worked on his estate. He was an idealist and a thinker, deeply interested in theosophy and spiritualism; he held the belief that all men were fundamentally good. He wrote a book criticizing the dictatorship and suggesting it was time we had a more democratic way of government. All the young intellectuals, like my father, were becoming impatient and restive, and Madero had something which, at that time in Mexico, was like a ray of light in a dark place—he had a fanatical devotion to an honest ideal—and there had been nothing like that since Benito Juárez!

'Almost overnight Madero found himself surrounded by followers, regarded as an apostle for freedom. Porfirio Díaz was alarmed naturally. He threw him into jail—but that only made him more popular. At last Madero escaped to the border. There, on 20th November 1910, he raised the flag of Revolution. When Madero made that Revolution he did not want to gain power for himself, only to bring back the Reforms of Juárez. By chance it was exactly a hundred years, all but two months, since the Revolution of Hidalgo had gained us our Independence from Spain. And so, when he was eighty-two years old, and had been dictator for thirty years, Porfirio Díaz was forced to abdicate. His last throw was that he left Corral, one of his friends, as puppet President. "He is a weak nice man," thought Porfirio, "and I will stand on his shadow!"

'But my father, who was heart and soul behind Madero, went into the Chamber of Deputies—which he called his battleground —and made speeches saying, "Here comes the phantom of Porfirio Díaz! What battles has he won? What medals does he own? Who *is* this incredibly charming patriotic gentleman?"—and just swept the floor with him. Within a few days Corral had disappeared. Then my father went on fighting for Madero. But though Madero was a great and a good man—the best man on earth for his intentions—he was not strong enough for such a gigantic task. He became President, but on 22nd February 1913, he was betrayed and murdered during a terrible siege of the National Palace, and Huerta became President. But my father could not be displaced as a member of the House of Deputies because his time was not yet up, and he would dash to the Chamber of Deputies and make impassioned speeches against Huerta. Sometimes two or three of Huerta's men would lie in wait for him. Then the ushers would whisper, "Señor Urueta—four men are waiting outside to kill you!", and he would jump out of the window and leave by the roof. This happened often.

'One day the owner of a store rushed out into the street and told him, "Don't go to your own house—they are waiting there for you!" So father sent a message to my mother, "Look for me in my brother's house," and hid there for a time. But finally Huerta trapped him at our house in Insurgentes. There were pine trees and his men hid there and caught my father as he walked up the path. He was thrown into a car and taken to Huerta who took him into his garden and there begged my father to speak for his side.

' "I will give you anything," he said, "lands . . . mines . . ." He told my father he could leave a fortune to each one of his children. "Build up their future now," he urged. "Ask me for anything you wish."

' "I have only one treasure to give my children," answered father, "and that is a clean name. So you see, I cannot accept your offer."

'And then he made Huerta a personal speech which so fascinated and hypnotized him that at the end he opened the door and said, "Get out quickly, by God, because my desire is to kill you— and I cannot do it at this moment!"

'Father ran home quickly. "We must go *now*," he said to my mother, and in no time they had packed and left by the roof, leaving grandmother to take care of the children. Within ten minutes a group of ten soldiers with bayonets arrived to kill him, and searched the house.

'After that, for six months, he was hidden in the cellar of a cousin. Cordelia and one of my brothers used to take him food and clothing and made out that he was in Europe. There was no light or fresh air in the cellar and gradually his health weakened.

'Finally, Huerta was extradited from Mexico and Carranza came to power and my father was made Under-Secretary of State. But very soon, in 1917, he resigned from that post realizing he could not help the Government, or his country, by sitting in an office, and went back to his battlefield—the Chamber of Deputies. Later there came a strong epidemic of influenza in Mexico. Father caught it and was terribly ill. Afterwards he was sent as Ambassador to Buenos Aires. He died while he was there. There was a big memorial service for him and then his body was brought back to Mexico. There was a big funeral here and he was buried in the place where the Mexican heroes are buried—La Rotunda de los Hombres Ilustres. There you have the story of my father and his speeches,' finished Margarita.

Sometime, somewhere, there comes to each of us a moment of awakening, of seeing the whole instead of the part. It is always a wonderful moment, whether in relation to a place, a person, or to life itself. From that day onwards, as I walked down Reforma . . . through Avendida Juárez . . . into Madero . . . across the Plaza de Jesús Urueta . . . the very stones spoke to me of what had been.

I saw things now in quite a different light. Often since my arrival I had come across scenes of such unbelievable poverty that they had haunted me—potholed streets running with sewage where whole families lived crowded into dark windowless one-room apartments; even more wretched hovels of sacking and tarred paper sometimes encamped against the very walls that hid some paradise of tree and flower. Now I saw suddenly how much was being done to overcome them. I would see a couple of school-girls in neat clean uniforms come running laughing down one of these slum-like streets and vanish into one of the squalid homes, and my heart would lift, for here already was growth. The Mexican Government puts aside a large portion of its budget for such education; the difficulty is that with such a prolific population it is hard to provide enough teachers, let alone enough schools.

Mexico has so many other problems too. Water, scanty to begin with and uneven in distribution, is an ever-present one. Another is that so many of the raw materials on which her economy depends —things like vanilla, coffee, *henequen*, silver—are now being produced by other countries too. The sad thing is that she has a wealth of untapped natural resources which, if developed, could provide employment for all her population. Unfortunately this needs tremendous capital.

Yet, when a country has been torn apart internally as often as

The church at Mitla built on the ruins of an ancient Indian palace

Fruit-sellers in the market at Acatlán

Wooden donkey-saddles and *petate* mats for sale in Acatlán

Silver-making at Taxco

Tortilla maker on the street corner, Ixtapalapa

Chamula Indians shopping in San Cristóbal de las Casas, Chiapas

Mexico has during her struggles for independence, complete new growth *cannot* be achieved overnight. It is a matter of time, for the growth of nations is part of the whole spiritual evolution of man in the Cosmos.

CHAPTER 7

ANTONIO'S WEDDING

A STIR was caused about this time by Antonio's announcement that he was getting married. Would the Señora honour him by being his *madrina* (godmother)—it being customary at a Mexican wedding to have a *madrina* for both bride and groom. A few days later there arrived for Margarita's inspection an elaborate affair of silk and lace, together with shoes and many small sprays of artificial flowers, as it is the duty of the groom to provide the bride's dress.

Two days before the wedding I arrived home to find Margarita with her leg encased in plaster. She made a wry face.

'Just after you went out this morning—a bicycle came too fast. I have to stay like this for three weeks!'

'Oh, what bad luck,' I began, then—'Goodness—the wedding!'

Margarita's eyes twinkled. 'It's all right, everything is arranged. I have talked it over with Antonio. *You* are going to be proxy godmother!'

'Me!' I exclaimed. 'But . . .'

'Don't worry, you'll manage—your Spanish is coming along nicely! You have only to dress the bride and place the *lassoo* over them in church. Look!' She picked up a silken cord in the shape of a huge bow. 'When the priest has married them you must stand behind and put this over their heads. Then take a corner of the bride's veil and place it round Antonio's shoulder—and somehow make it stay there, for if it slips off it will bring bad luck to the marriage! Afterwards there will be a wedding feast and being the *madrina* you will be the guest of honour. Be careful with the *tequila*! It is very strong—and there will be a lot as it is a village wedding. Now I must find you a veil. In that drawer you will see several. Yes, there in the corner is my nice lace one!'

It occurred to me then that I did not even know where the village was, let alone how to get there—but even that was all arranged.

'A *camionetta* is going to take the wedding guests from Mexico City tomorrow evening at eight o'clock and it will pick you up here,' explained Margarita. 'Antonio says it is about seven hours from the city so you should reach the village about four o'clock in the morning. He has already left. The wedding will be at eleven o'clock in the morning and the *camionetta* will return in the evening.'

At eight o'clock next evening I was waiting armed with the precious cardboard box containing the bride's *vestido*. By eight-thirty there was still no sign of the *camionetta*, nor by nine o'clock; being used to the time lag in Mexico by now this did not worry me. At half-past nine Mina came running into the library to announce breathlessly that it was outside. Margarita hobbled out with me, balancing precariously on a pair of crutches.

The back of the *camionetta* (a small open truck) had been trans-formed into a sort of cave with poles, ropes and canvas. However, as the *madrina* and guest of honour, I was installed in the cab beside the driver. With a wave to Margarita and Mina at the gate we drove off into the night to collect the various relatives, and the next three hours were spent hooting the horn or knocking at doors in the poorer parts of Mexico City. Each time, more bundles, *petate* mats and baskets were carried out and loaded in the back and the truck rocked back and forth as everybody eased themselves round by the light of matches. At last, with fifteen people in the back and three in front, we swayed off into the dark-ness. We stopped once more, this time on a corner where a woman was steaming *tamales* in an old drum and frying *enchilladas*; every-body climbed back into the truck clutching a steaming maize packet or a juicy *enchillada* dripping with hot lard and bulging with onion and chile.

We had not been going long before it was discovered that the lights had stopped working. Out came a bag of tools, and the driver and several male cousins disappeared for a while under the bonnet.

There was no untoward incident after this, apart from the fact that we nearly ran over the legs of a man stretched out in the gutter as if dead. The driver shook his head reprovingly. 'Too much *pulque*! He will sleep there till morning!'

One of the female cousins, with a baby wrapped in her *rebozo*, was in front with me, and we huddled down together as the truck began to gather speed and the night wind cut through the cab, for since there was no cap to the petrol tank, only some old rag, it was necessary that all the windows should be open to prevent the driver being overcome by fumes.

Huge trailers began to pass us on their way into the city to the early morning market, and, being on the outside, we skidded blindly round the hairpin bends with headlights blazing full at us and a precipice a few inches away.

Soon we left all habitation behind except for an occasional *adobe* village where moonlight glinted on a blue or yellow dome. It must have been about three o'clock in the morning, when the driver, who had been driving more and more erratically, swerved to a standstill and announced that he could drive no further without sleep. There was an argument as to whether it would be better to restore him with a good drink from the bottle of some strong alcohol, which was now being passed round in the back, or let him sleep for half an hour. In the end it was decided that the latter was perhaps wiser under the circumstances. Stretched out on the cab seat, he slept sonorously for the next half hour while the moonlit road became a study in stretching and yawning figures, many not altogether too steady on their feet.

In the moonlight that wild countryside was a place of enchantment. I wandered up the road till the truck was lost from sight. Silence engulfed me and I might have strayed into another sphere. Great rocks stood out like pillars on the mountainside. Everywhere, silhouetted needle-sharp against the moonlit sky, were great organ cacti, their majestic clusters of olive-green pipes moonlit to blackness. The whole hillside resembled some astral cathedral patiently awaiting the passing from earth of another Bach to set the gorges trembling and thundering.

When I returned to the track I found the driver being shaken protestingly into wakefulness. However after water had been splashed over his face and head he announced that he felt able to continue.

It was half-past seven before we pulled up in the square of a little village. The female cousin and I, who felt very well acquainted having spent the night huddled together against the onslaught of petrol fumes and icy winds, looked at each other delightedly and prepared to untangle ourselves and the baby from the folds of my plastic raincoat and her *rebozo* which had combined to keep us all warm. In the square, one woman had already opened a stall, and it soon became obvious that this was the only reason for our stop, for the entire company, red-eyed from lack of sleep, their clothes crumpled, crowded round her holding out twenty-*centavo* pieces, and receiving in exchange a steaming *tortilla* piled with raw meat, onion and chile. Apparently we were still miles from our destination.

The sun was now very hot so the canvas cover was ripped off and one of the male cousins, well fortified by raw meat *tacos* and the night's alcohol, came and installed himself beside me at the wheel.

The road was now just a track between fields. Even this soon came to an end at a dry river bed which we negotiated with difficulty, and there now appeared nothing but steep slopes of broken rock ahead. However, the driver, after crossing himself four times, let in the clutch and we lurched upwards. A steep gorge dropped away on one side and the track, when visible at all, was no wider than the wheels of the truck, and sometimes so rough as to wrench the steering wheel right round. The company in the back were now clinging on to each other, sweating as much with fright as with the heat, crossing themselves, and calling out to the driver to stop whenever we slid so near the edge that we almost slid over. Had he not been so well fortified with the night's alcohol I think even he might have lost his nerve, but, as it was, apart from another hasty sign of the cross or an occasional appeal to the Holy Virgin pinned on the windscreen, he kept his foot on the accelerator. The track was really only for donkeys, and occasionally we met two or three heavily loaded, their owner walking beside them. Each time there would be a great to-do, the donkeys having to be shoved and pushed off the track down the rough hillside, much to the annoyance of their owner and peril of their loads.

Sometimes at a cutting through a canyon the driver had to get out and push aside great lumps of rock left by some recent land-slide. However at last he pulled up, and putting his head out of the window gave a wild shout. The village was in sight! It lay far below, a cluster of *adobe* and plaster houses and a white church, set in a cactus-sprinkled valley. One more wide dry river, and then we were careering down a steep track into the village. At the sound figures came running from all directions, including Antonio who had been expecting us since four o'clock and as it was now nine was convinced we must have gone over a precipice.

Everyone having embraced each other, we were taken into the yard of a small grey *adobe* house and directed into a bamboo hut where a large mattress had been spread on the earth floor. The thatch roof, which had a hole at either end for light and ventila-tion, was supported by tree trunks tied with cords; brown pottery jugs of many sizes, decorated with a simple black design, hung all round on nails. The door was just some bamboo sticks strung together with string and looped back, while a pole thrust across one corner of the wall served as a wardrobe. One end of the hut was taken up by a basket, eight feet high, holding maize; it had a small opening at the bottom plugged with a cork; nearby stood a heap of small black beans and two large kerosene water tins.

Into this room the guests all crowded. Bundles, boxes, *petate* mats and clothing, were carried in after us and we all got down to the serious business of dressing for the wedding. A brown earthen-

[74]

ware bowl of water was put on the floor and into this everyone dipped their hands and washed their faces, the men rubbing the water over their hair too, and drying their hands on their shirt tails. Occasionally a lean dog, all ribs, wandered in under the screen of legs and clothes and managed to lap a few drops out of the bowl before it was discovered and chased out. When the water got too dirty it was thrown out of the door and some more poured out of one of the kerosene tins.

I hurried into my dress, which I had carried in the cardboard box with the bride's, then squeezed my way with a repeated, 'Con permiso', through the robing and disrobing figures, and went anxiously in search of the bride since one of my main objects in being there was to get her dressed. I had met her for a brief moment on our arrival, presented her with the cardboard box, then lost sight of her again.

I found her in the outer room standing by a long wooden table, which, with three benches, was the only furniture. On the table was spread the wedding dress, rather creased after its night in the box. She was smoothing it out with a large unwieldy iron containing smoking fragments of charcoal.

'Josefina!' I exclaimed. '*You* mustn't be doing that! Let me do it for you.'

I took the iron from her and worked my way round the skirt, watched by a number of villagers gathered in the gap in the earth wall that served as a window.

'There!' I exclaimed, at last thankful to have finished before we were both overcome by the charcoal fumes. 'Now where are *you* going to dress?'

For answer Josefina smiled and led the way back into the hut where the earth floor was now well churned up by milling feet and strewn with the discarded clothing of guests still in various stages of dress and undress. I managed to clear a space to spread out a *petate* mat for her to stand on and fresh water was put into the pottery bowl for her. It was now discovered that there was no petticoat in the box but one of the guests obligingly took off her dress again and removed her own which, though a trifle crushed and grubby from the night's journeying, served the purpose. At this point a dog fight began outside, and as most of the guests hurried out either to see it or to stop it, we were able to get down to the serious business of the dress, the shoes and the veil in peace, apart from four or five small boys at the open door who were watching every step with interest. The final touch was the little artificial flower sprays which all had to be fastened on somewhere—one over each ear, one on each shoe and the remainder on the veil. When at last I had finished, Josefina, with her big dark eyes and her black hair combed out loosely under the veil, was as pretty a bride as you could wish to see.

She explained that she must now receive her women guests formally, so with the aid of a few aunts and cousins I quickly piled all the baskets and clothes at one end. Then while somebody went to find a kitchen chair, I raked the floor over and shook the earth off the *petate* mat. We then set the chair in the middle of it and installed the bride on it. She sat there very upright and solemn while the women guests, in best clothes and *rebozos*, came in one by one to congratulate her. This small ceremony was just ending when we heard church bells, and a voice from a loudspeaker on the roof announced that the wedding of Antonio and Josefina would shortly begin. This was the signal for all the guests to rush off to the church and soon the room was empty except for the bride, myself and the second godmother.

But meantime all was activity outside in the yard under the shady *mesquite* tree where the women from the village were hard at work preparing the wedding feast. A friend of the bridegroom's who had volunteered to keep the fires going went back and forth continually with faggots of *mesquite* wood.

On the fires, which were built between three stones, stood huge *cazuelas* (earthenware pots) blackened with use. In the largest was the *mole poblano* (turkey in hot sauce), always the chief item at a Mexican wedding. Because it contains so many ingredients (twenty-four in all—among them such unlikely partners as tomatoes, garlic, almonds, sesame seeds, cinnamon, fried onions, cloves and unsweetened chocolate to which sugar is added)—and most of these have to be fried, baked or toasted and then ground separately before being mixed together and cooked slowly for about fifteen hours in the skimmed broth in which the turkey has been cooked, this dish takes a day or two to prepare. The turkey had now been cut into small pieces and added to the rich dark creamy sauce and was just having its last couple of hours' cooking to be ready when we came out of church.

On the adjoining fire stood a large *olla* (a narrow-necked earthenware pot), full of black beans boiling with salt, onion and cloves; now that they had boiled one of the women was adding a few spoonfuls of lard to make them a little greasy. (In every Mexican household there is always such a pot of beans cooking and if an unexpected guest comes the remark is, 'Well, we can always put some water with the beans!')

The little yard was bounded by spikes of organ cactus stuck in the soft ground in place of a fence, and through the gaps, the brown eyes of six cows tethered on the other side stared unblinkingly at the cooks.

Two women came into the yard, each carrying gracefully on her shoulder a pottery bowl of yellow *masa* (maize dough). Two of the cooks quickly began making *tortillas* of it. One of them, her mauve skirt topped with an orange blouse, and her pigtails secured by red ribbon, began to knead the dough vigorously on her curved slab of volcanic stone, rolling it so fine with her stone rolling pin that I could see the blue-black pattern of the stone through the yellow paste. When she had made a little heap she passed it across to her companion who slapped it back and forth between the palms of her hands till it was like a thin round pancake, flapping it in the air a few times before dropping it on to the round iron *comal*. After a while the *tortilla* would begin to rise a little, like bubblegum. Once it was flecked with brown on both sides she would toss it into a lined basket which she kept covered with a cloth.

Water was being brought in continually, either by donkeys with huge brown jars strapped to their wooden saddles, or by a man with a pole across his shoulders from which dangled two rusty kerosene tins. An old woman wrapped in a *rebozo* sat like a statue cross-legged on the ground by the water jars, her duty being to keep off the dogs and pigs that kept trying to get their heads into the mouths of the jars or lick the wet ropes.

All this time we continued to sit in stately silence in the small hut waiting for the summons to church, the other godmother and myself reclining on the mattress on the floor.

At last a small boy rushed in to announce that the priest was ready. As we passed through the door the bride turned to me with a sweet smile. Indicating the little room with its churned-up earth floor and its miscellany of discarded clothing she said graciously, '*Es su casa, señorita!*'

We set out in a little procession, the bride first with her father— a big man in a striped shirt—and myself next wearing Margarita's veil and carrying the silk *lassoo*. At the same moment a small procession emerged from another *adobe* house. It was the bridegroom dressed in a black suit, the bottom of his trousers secured firmly by cycle clips, and his best man close behind him. Men raised their hats as we passed, as if at a funeral, and the entire village crowded into the church behind us.

At the door the priest gave a short discourse. Then the best man brought out the ring for inspection, and Antonio produced a tiny gilt box containing coins, symbolizing all his wealth. There was a slight delay because neither he nor the priest could open this, but finally, after it was passed round among the by-standers, someone discovered how the spring worked. Some Holy Water was brought, a flower dipped into it, and with this the priest sprinkled Antonio, Josefina, the ring and the little box, while small barefooted boys dodged under the arms of their elders to get a better view.

We then sorted ourselves into a procession and followed him up the church, which was quite empty except for two or three benches at the top. Those of us immediately concerned knelt down on the stone floor while the rest of the congregation settled themselves comfortably on the floor against the walls. One tiny boy climbed up on the altar rails and sat there swinging his bare feet until reprimanded by the server who, in a bright pink shirt, his cotton trousers secured with tape at the ankles, was endeavouring to cope with a large brass cross, a lighted taper and a smoking censer all at the same time and wanted no more distractions. The organist, in a *zarape*, his sandalled feet pedalling away for dear life on the small harmonium, was so enthusiastic that he went on playing silently with his fingers even when he was not actually required.

During the long sermon small children began to totter about the church, occasionally going down with a thud as they unexpectedly encountered the legs of a member of the congregation. One guest had resourcefully folded his *zarape* in two and was kneeling on that; I cast envious glances at him as, by this time, the stone floor was getting rather hard; another, unable to see too well, was pushing his straw hat ahead of him round the floor as he eased himself towards a more favourable position.

Nudged at the right moment by relatives, I rose with my *lassoo* and stationed myself behind the bride and groom. Draping the end of Josefina's veil carefully round Antonio's shoulder (and surreptitiously tucking it under his coat collar, for I was taking no chances on having it fall off to bring bad luck on the entire wedding) I slipped the *lassoo* neatly over the two heads. Thus awkwardly linked, the pair rose unsteadily. The dangerous moment passed—the veil remained in place. The server in the pink shirt now picked up a wooden wheel in which were set a great many bells and began shaking it back and forth energetically. The final hymn was sung; I removed the *lassoo*, handed it with a bow to the bride, and the ceremony was at an end.

Back at the house a table had been set up with bottles of beer and Coca-Cola. Two guitarists, squatting on their heels in a corner, struck up a cross between a waltz and a polka and bride and groom had the first dance, her silk dress trailing on the dusty earth floor; I was invited to have the next dance with the bridegroom. As fresh crates of beer were opened bottle tops spun down like sycamore keys and were soon trodden into the earth floor.

After about an hour of drinking and dancing it was time for the wedding feast. The long wooden table on which I had done the ironing was now set with bowls of steaming soup and piles of *tortillas*. Since all could not sit down at once with the limited accommodation, this 'first sitting' was for the bride and groom, the godparents and immediate relatives, and such V.I.P.s as the President of the Village. The 'second sitting' crowded round to watch us eat, while as many of the village as could do so crammed themselves into the window space, climbing on one another's shoulders to get a better view, and enjoying the feast vicariously from the steaming spicy odours.

The cooks, perspiring from their labours, came in bearing more pots of chicken and lentil soup . . . more *tortillas*. The latter, each the size of a soup-plate, were slapped down in steaming piles on the wooden table and came in useful for everything.

With our fingers we would pick out a piece of hot chicken from our soup, wrap it in a torn-off scrap of *tortilla*, and eat it; another scrap, folded over, was used to scoop up the liquid since the only spoons were the huge wooden ones used for stirring the pots; the remainder of the *tortilla* was used as a napkin to wipe one's mouth before being finally eaten.

After the soup, huge *cazuelas* of the rich brown *mole poblano* were brought in, flanked on either side by bowls of steaming mauve-black 'beans of the pot'. But before anyone helped themselves—and I was very touched by this—a special bowl of white turkey meat, without any sauce, was put in front of me in case, being a foreigner, I was not addicted to things *picante*.

Also, since I might not yet be partial to *tortillas*, a plate of violently pink cakes was placed near me as an alternative. (As a matter of fact I much preferred *tortillas*—somehow turkey and pink cakes just don't go together.)

As the main occupation of the village is hat weaving most of the guests had brought their current hat, and those not yet eating went on working in order not to waste time. As the onlookers at the window were also working on *their* hats, the effect of fingers and straws in continuous movement all round us was a little disturbing to the digestion. After the turkey came bowls of

The Wedding Speeches

chicken and pork, green *mole* made with green tomatoes and chiles, and red *mole* made with ripe tomatoes. Meanwhile from under the table came a continual growling as half a dozen lean dogs prowled about, pushing against our legs. Occasionally the table would rock violently as they started to fight over a dropped *tortilla* or a flung down turkey bone, churning up the earth floor as they did so and sending up a cloud of dust over the nearest diners. Everybody would shout and kick at them and they would rush out one after the other knocking over any guests who happened to be in the way.

When nothing remained but a few *tortillas*, a bottle of *tequila* was passed round and a toast proposed to the bride and groom. Antonio was pushed to his feet to reply which he did very bashfully. The President of the Village, lean faced, in open-necked shirt and sandals, rose next. He talked about Antonio bringing honour to his village by having an English godmother—here he bowed deeply in my direction; of the union in this wedding of the city and the country. He took another gulp of *tequila* and grew more eloquent, clenched his fists and talked of the Sons of the Village . . . the Sacrifices . . . the *Conquistadores* . . . the Revolution . . . the Country—and sat down amidst applause, the uninvited guests half in and half out of the window clapping the loudest of all.

I was now called upon to give a speech, and though my Spanish was undeniably shaky it obviously served the purpose, for I, too, sat down to loud applause.

Antonio, who had now had time for a good many gulps of *tequila*, now leapt to his feet again. He thanked his guests . . . the President . . . the Godmother from England . . . he thanked all the sons of the Village for their Sacrifices . . . and finally had to be helped back into his chair with tears streaming down his cheeks.

Guest after guest now leapt to their feet and the speeches grew more and more eloquent, if more and more disjointed. Antonio was embraced repeatedly by the guest on his right and on his left, but I noticed nobody said a word about the bride.

[81]

Meantime, as Antonio had paid to have a record player and a loudspeaker on the roof announcing his wedding and playing continuous music, this was going on unabated overhead.

It was now realized that half the guests were as yet unfed. People began to rise a little unsteadily; the women came in, cleared away the bowls and threw any half-eaten *tortillas* under the table to the dogs; the remainder of the guests seated themselves ravenously, and the whole thing began all over again. By the time it was ended a stupor fell over the entire wedding party. Guests wandered off to unroll their *petate* mats in any meagre patches of shade; the women went on for a while making more *tortillas*, their slap-slap forming a rhythmic background to the snores of the men, then they too retired for a siesta.

In the hut in which we had dressed, *petate* mats were spread out on every available inch of the earth floor and the big mattress was filled to overflowing with as many as could fit on to it. I was given a mat on the floor beside the maize basket and was soon fast asleep.

After a couple of hours first one and then another began to stir and yawn, and when we emerged into the sunlight again we found that a band, consisting of a couple of guitars, a drum and a gourd had arrived and were installed in the room where we had feasted. The table had been removed, benches pushed back against the wall, and the floor raked over and sprinkled with water. The first dance was a *ranchero* dance and for this some of the men donned wide cowboy trousers. They danced with their hands behind their backs stamping up to a girl and circling round her in slow motion, the dance gradually working up to a tempestuous finish. As the *tequila* bottle was passed round the dancing grew wilder, and dust filled the room from stamping feet—sandalled, bare or booted. Those not dancing went on diligently weaving their hats so that the whole room was one continuous movement of fingers, straw, legs and feet. Dogs yelped as they darted in and out amongst the dancers in search of any *tortilla* which might have got buried. The bride, her finery now a little wilted, still sat upright on a hard chair, for traditionally she does no work

all day but is waited on. Anyone passing by in the street automatically stopped to join the onlookers jammed in the window
space.

Some of the guests now decided to go down to the village
baseball pitch. The Mexicans, as a whole, are very keen on baseball and football; they are also exuberant spectators, and during a
match anything from lighted paper bags to beer bottles and cakes
may be thrown from the stands.

I was thinking with longing by this time of a quiet half-hour
alone on some hilltop. With this in mind, I slipped out with the
rest but made my way in the opposite direction to where an
earth track led out of the village.

'Señorita! Señorita!'

I heard someone calling urgently, and turning round saw the
female cousin of the night before hurrying after me. Four men
who had apparently been coming in the same direction had
stopped in their tracks and were watching her narrowly. She
caught up with me.

'Not alone, señorita!' she said in a low voice. 'Better I come with
you—but better we go the other way to the baseball where is
more people.'

She walked back past the men as if they did not exist. I could see
by their unsteady gait that they had been drinking heavily and
recognized them as some of the onlookers at the window.

The baseball pitch was just a clearing among the cacti, for the
whole village was literally 'carved out' from a cactus valley, and
its few narrow earth streets were lined on both sides with organ
cactus, sometimes twenty feet high, giving the appearance of
gigantic green fences.

Here on the baseball pitch the players had hung their straw hats
on the cactus spikes so that they looked like some incongruous
type of flower. We soon tired of the baseball and instead wandered
from one gigantic *nopal* cactus to another knocking down the
tender new disc-like leaves with a stick and gathering them into
her *rebozo* since they would come in useful to our host for a cactus
relish for supper.

Back in the house we found a heated argument going on. Guests who had expected to return to Mexico City that evening now found that no one was capable of driving over that mountain track. Finally it was decided that we must all stay the night and leave early in the morning.

By this time, what with the dust, the heat, the thirst engendered by the *tortillas* and the hot *mole*, not to mention all the fizzy drinks since I had confined myself to Coca-Cola, my greatest longing was for a cup of tea. Luckily I had my jar of Instant Tea and a tin mug with me. I filled it from one of the big brown water pots, set it on one of the fires, and when it boiled, carried it over to the big tree in the middle of the maize field and sat leaning against the trunk. Above me the huge fork of the tree, which served as a maize loft, was crammed with gold dry straw. One of the guests in a nigger-brown *zarape* came over with a pitchfork, and with a 'Con permiso, señorita', pulled some down to feed the various donkeys, who hurried over, crunching it up and sucking up any little bits of maize leaf from the dusty ground as neatly as vacuum cleaners. When I asked him what he thought the time was, my watch having stopped, he looked up at the sun, measured the lengthening shadows with his eye, and gave me what I imagine was a perfectly correct answer.

A young girl of about fourteen, barefooted, slender, her old black *rebozo* making a lovely frame for her dark eyes, came over and squatted on her heels beside me, her fingers weaving briskly in and out of a half-made hat, a bundle of fresh straw tucked under her arm.

'Is it difficult?' I asked.

'You can't make a hat?' she exclaimed incredulously—*she* had been making hats since she was six years old. Deftly she picked out some fresh strands and began a new one to demonstrate, her fingers flying back and forth so fast that I could hardly follow. She told me proudly that she could make two hats a day, and sent twelve to the market each week.

As dusk fell a man came out into the yard with a paraffin lantern and hung it up on a branch of the tree; women got up

Antonio's wedding . . . the streets of the village were lined with tall cacti
Antonio and his bride and some of the wedding guests

Outside in the yard the cooks were preparing the wedding feast

After the feast. The guests retired with their *petate* mats for a siesta

from the shadows and began fanning the embers of the fires with old *tortillas* or roughly made fans of green palm. Dishes were wiped out with lettuce leaves ready for the next meal, and the baskets of left-over food lifted down from forks of the tree where they had been lodged for safety from the dogs and pigs. Huge pots of water were put on to boil for the chocolate which was frothed up in special wooden chocolate pots by means of a wooden stick with loose rings on it which was spun back and forth between the palms of the hands.

The bridegroom's friend who had spent the day bringing faggots for the fires had carried his half-finished hat on his head all day and in between his duties had managed to get quite a lot done, so now there was twice as much hat on his head as when I first saw him.

The long table was set up in the yard with a few pieces of stone wedged underneath to stop the legs sinking in the dust. On it were placed *tortillas*, fresh or reheated, sprinkled with chile and salt; a big dish of refried beans—this morning's 'beans of the pot' crushed and fried, then patted into an oblong block and sprinkled with grated cheese; and thick pottery mugs of the strong frothy chocolate.

(Maize, in the form of *tortillas*, small black beans and green *chile* are the main diet of the Mexican Indian today as they were in Aztec days. In some combination or other they are eaten at practically every meal in poorer households. Except on a feast day like this, breakfast consists of the cheap Mexican coffee—coffee beans ground with burnt sugar—and a few *tortillas*; lunch is usually *tortillas*, boiled beans and chile; and supper is *tortillas* again with mashed refried beans and chile, plus a mug of hot chocolate. Actually it is a very healthy diet because maize contains carbohydrates and calcium, beans are full of protein, and the green chile peppers are rich in Vitamin C.)

A little group gathered round the fire and began to tell me something of the life of their village. They were all Mixtec Indians and proud of it for theirs had been one of the great cultures of early America. Their ancestors were among the most accomplished artists in goldwork. The greatest treasure of gold jewellery yet found in America—in the famous Tomb No. 7 at Monte Albán in Oaxaca—was of Mixtec origin, and among the most precious of the *Codices* (picture-writing records on skin or fibre) which survived destruction by the Spaniards are seven recording Mixtec history from the Creation onwards.

They told me they speak Mixteca among themselves, though they use Spanish elsewhere, and were delighted when I learnt some phrases (phonetically I'm afraid—I had no idea of the spelling)— '*Too-noo varnay*', Good day; '*Ensay varnay*', Thank you and '*Ah kay nay*', How are you? There are still about sixty different Indian languages spoken in Mexico. Most of the men were clean-shaven, unlike the more Spanish element of the city where a small toothbrush moustache is characteristic.

Today these descendants of the famous Mixtec goldsmiths are hatweavers. Several hundred hats go from this village to the market every week to sell there for one *peso* fifty *centavos* (about 10*d.*), and later in Mexico City for five *pesos*. Most families have their own little maize field which provides them with *tortillas* all the year round. Since most travelling and carrying of water is done by donkey most families own one or more. A little bus also comes through periodically. (There is nearly always a bus, however old and ramshackle, that plies between these remote villages, especially on market days. Loaded down inside and out with its weight of passengers, baskets, bundles, pigs and chickens it will bump and rattle its way over almost impossible mountain tracks.)

At supper I was given the seat of honour at the head of the crowded table. All round on the dusty ground of the yard little groups sat in the fire and lantern-flickered darkness with their mugs of chocolate. Behind us the *adobe* and bamboo walls were vague and shadowy; above, stars glittered intermittently through the feathery lamplit branches of the *mesquite* tree, and streaks of moonlight dappled the gaunt cactus fence.

Suddenly I noticed a small procession coming awkwardly across the moonlit maize field. It was four men carrying on their shoulders an old iron bedstead and a mattress. This was for the godmother from England! With great difficulty it was pushed through the narrow opening into the small room where we had danced, the floor of which by this time was a mosaic pattern of bare feet, boots and sandals—plus the footmarks of the dogs, pigs and chickens which had been wandering in and out all day.

When we returned to the yard, a fresh crate of beer had been opened and the bottle of *tequila* was being passed round. A guitar was produced and the player seated himself next to me and began to pluck at the strings. From the shadows first one voice then another would begin a verse, then everyone would join in the chorus, harmonizing perfectly together. Some sang with their eyes closed, others did nothing more than contribute an occasional groan.

Figures drifting in from the streets to listen were visible only as white rims of hats. Some squatted down on their heels against the wall, *zarapes* pulled round them, others stretched out full-length on the ground, hats over their eyes, their legs in the narrow white cotton trousers glimmering in the firelight. Everyone had relaxed except the dogs, which still kept up their unwearied search for food. It must have been about half-past ten but it was still not cold; I was quite warm with just a cardigan over my summer frock.

The glowing embers of the fires; the sharp silhouettes of the tall cacti; the lean brown cheeks high-lighted by the lantern; the shower of sparks as someone flicked a cigarette end into the darkness; the dark shining eyes of the women, who sat for the most part in the shadows, their *rebozos* pulled across their mouths against the night air . . . I might have been looking at a Diego Rivera mural.

One song which was called for again and again was *Corazon* (Heart), a lilting romantic tune; but most of the songs had a melancholy strain, though the saddest was liable to be interrupted unexpectedly by a high wail, or end in a series of shouts.

Our original driver, after a long drink at a bottle of fiery *mescal*, suddenly surprised everyone by bursting into song in a rich deep voice. The guitarist, who had been playing to himself in a state of self-induced hypnosis, his forehead almost on the strings, looked up, startled, and began to play with renewed zest; the two of them went off into a magnificent duet, their eyes fixed on each other's faces, oblivious to everyone. Shouts of bravo came from all round; the two were plied with more *tequila*, more *mescal*, and the rhythm began to increase in intensity. Songs began to be interrupted more and more frequently by wild screams, startling the small moths which were circling round the lantern, and sending them flickering up into the branches like showers of stars. Verses became interminable and at the end the singer would be almost weeping with emotion. Occasionally a shawled figure would enter silent-footed from the street, tap one of the recumbent figures peremptorily, and, after some remonstrance, he would get up and follow her reluctantly, lingering and looking back all the way.

A woman with long black pigtails had been detailed to sleep with me on the iron bedstead as a chaperone and at last she and I departed to our 'bedroom', the rest of the women guests unrolling their *petate* mats on the floor of the hut in which we had dressed. We settled down one each end of the bare mattress, I wrapped in my coat, she in an old *zarape*, the only light being the moonlight which flooded in through the opening that served as a door.

Outside the singing went on unabated, the voices becoming increasingly emotional till at last it sounded exactly like a chorus of cats wailing on a wall. Suddenly there came a chorus of answering wails from some group who must have been sitting in the street outside under the 'window'—now partially blocked by a thin screen of plaited bamboo. This duet of wailing continued hour after hour. The guitar, on the other hand, improving with every moment, had become a throbbing undertone of almost intoxicating vibrancy.

Occasionally I would hear a soft shuffle of feet, the moonlight would be blotted out, and a dark figure would stagger in, drop his *machete* knife on the earth floor with a thud, and then follow it; in a few moments he would be fast asleep. Sometimes someone would wander in and grope among the piles of empty bottles in the corner in case a full one might have been missed, before he too slumped on the floor.

I was almost asleep too—and just congratulating myself that though it was intensely hot in the now rather overcrowded room at least there were no mosquitoes—when I felt a stealthy movement on the bed, and opening one eye, saw my companion sitting up. She listened for a moment, apparently to make sure I was asleep, then, satisfied, slid cautiously off the bed. Stepping noiselessly over the many inert bodies that now strewed the floor, she disappeared into the moonlight. There came a sudden lull in the wailing, then a fresh clink of bottles; when it started up again, a high female voice predominated! After about a quarter of an hour she crept noiselessly back on to the bed together with a strong smell of *mescal*.

It had been decided overnight that the truck must depart by six in the morning before the heat grew too intense, and with the first streak of daylight I awoke to find four men bending over two of the prone figures on the floor, shaking them vigorously, and repeating 'You must! You must!' However, our potential drivers, buried under their *zarapes*, refused to stir except to mutter that they could not and would not.

The four gave up at last and went out arguing among themselves, but already people were emerging bleary-eyed from their diverse resting places, rolling up their *petate* mats and laden with all their belongings under the impression that we were departing any minute for Mexico City. (I understand now why in Mexico a guest who overstays his welcome is referred to as 'staying even to pick up the *petate* mat'!)

A fire was fanned into flames, hot sweet coffee was boiled up, the remains of the *tortillas* reheated and, together with the remaining bottles of beer, set out on the table where one or two guests were still asleep, their heads down among the empty bottles. But by eight o'clock we were still sitting there. As it was now obvious that the drivers would need till at least eleven o'clock to sleep off the effects of the night, those male guests who were able, including the bridegroom, went off with shotguns to bring back something for a meal, while a band of women went off to the river to forage for fruit.

By now we had become a sort of open house for the whole village, and all the morning as the women slapped up more *tortillas*, men wandered in from the street, finishing up any half-bottles of beer that had been overlooked, or just squatting down by the fires, when one of the women would usually hand over a *tortilla* sprinkled with salt and chile. As the heat increased even the dogs ceased their interminable searching and lay about in scraps of shade in utter abandon looking like corpses. Only three brown and black pigs and a few leggy chickens continued to wander in and out of the house, while a hen, imprisoned under an upturned basket until she should lay an egg, clucked plaintively to announce that she might now be released.

The appointed hour of departure had come and gone long before the hunters returned, crowding into the yard with much noise and laughter, the sweat pouring from their faces, their shirts clinging damply to them, but disappointed because they had got nothing except one rabbit—and *that* someone had caught with their bare hands. A gourd was filled and refilled with water and they drank thirstily, throwing it over their heads as well and rubbing their hands through their black shiny hair. But the women had been more fortunate; they arrived back laden with enormous green water-melons, feathery sticks of sugar-cane six feet long, and great hands of bananas. These were carried triumphantly indoors. Two of the men took out their *machete* knives, and, while one chopped the sugar-cane into edible pieces, the other balanced a large water-melon on a chair and began to carve it into slices, the juice running down the chair legs as he did so and soaking into the earth floor.

A veritable feast followed as, sitting on benches, on the floor, or on the mattress—where the guns were lying still hot from the sun —we chewed at the sweet oozing sugar-cane and bit into huge slices of water-melon so ripe that the red juice dripped down my chin and even on to my ankles. By the time we had finished the floor was thickly littered with shiny black pips, green skin and chewed-up sugar-cane fibre.

I had discovered by this time that the house belonged, not to Antonio at all, but to a cousin who was away in Mexico City but who had obligingly lent it for the wedding. However even with forty or so guests this could be done with impunity since there were no windows to break, no furniture to spoil, no carpets to worry about—nothing, in fact, that a good rake up with a stiff palm brush, and a little vigorous throwing out of bottles, could not put right in half an hour.

As it was now far too hot to drive it was decided to postpone our departure till late afternoon; it was also decided—though reluctantly—that the *tequila* and *mescal* bottle had better be left severely alone by everybody if the guests were ever to get back to Mexico City at all. Accordingly nothing stronger than beer and Coca-Cola was opened this time but into this was crammed crushed ice for a whole block had arrived that morning by donkey and now lay on the floor wrapped in grass and a *petate* mat to keep it solid. Having now seen many such blocks of ice being dragged through dusty streets on the end of a rope I knew better than to be tempted. It can often be as fatal for the foreigner in Mexico to drink a bottled drink with ice as to drink the plain undrinkable water, and this was certainly neither the time nor the place to pro-voke an attack of 'turismo' (which is a glorified form of dysentery), since the sanitary arrangements were nil, being merely the bushes at the end of the maize field.

A meal was now prepared of old *tortillas* baked crisp, cut into strips and put into the remains of yesterday's broth; this was fol-lowed by refried beans, green *mole*, our cactus relish, and the rest of the pink cakes. As many as possible sat at the long table in the yard; the rest squatted on their heels in a wide circle round a *petate* mat spread with food, while the dogs, which seemed to have doubled in number since yesterday, formed a patient, but vigilant, outer circle.

The fresh air, the exercise, the fruit, the food—and above all the refraining from *tequila*—had now so revived the entire party that the speeches which followed might well have gone on into the evening again had not one of the older guests, gesticulating a little too enthusiastically, struck his head so violently against the wall that he split his scalp open and stood there with the blood streaming down his shirt. He was hurried off home by his relatives, protesting, and still finishing his speech in the street. This broke up the party, and the serious work of loading up the truck began.

All who were leaving went round embracing those who were not; I was embraced by everyone, not once but many times, and assured '*En su casa, señorita*' over and over again. By now so many people wanted a ride into the nearest market that the problem was to fit them all in. Those who could not get inside the truck arranged themselves along the running boards, including the President of the Village who, with several others armed with guns, planned to drop off half-way across the mountains and finish the day hunting. Just as we were about to move off he remembered that he had not written out Antonio's wedding lines therefore the civil marriage had not yet taken place; this was soon remedied with a piece of paper and a ball-point pen. Finally we went lurching up the steep cactus-lined street to a chorus of '*Adios! Adios!*'

At each river-bed and rocky gorge, everyone on the running boards had to dismount and run on ahead, while the driver, still rather shaky, and crossing himself a great many times, started off after them. Since, once started he had to keep going on the steep rocky inclines, and since the track was too narrow and precipitous for us to pass them, they had to run frantically to keep ahead of us, guns and *machete* knives bobbing up and down on their backs, and then jump back on to the running board and hang there by the roof, breathless and perspiring.

At last, having stopped once so that a woman in the back could lean out and embrace a cousin who was passing on a donkey, and a second time to let the hunters off at a desirable spot, we arrived in the little market place of Petlalcingo. Here we unloaded our surplus passengers and were embraced once more by all concerned. Then our wheels began to run smoothly on tarmac again, and we found ourselves back on the road to Mexico City.

CHAPTER 8

TO OAXACA AND CHIAPAS

IN THE SMALL TOWN of Acatlán I decided to get off the truck, find a room for the night, then make my way south to Oaxaca, and so climbed out to a chorus of 'Adios, señorita!'

In the hotel the small rooms opened off a centre patio and a swarthy man with a moustache directed me to Room No. 13, a tiny box-like room with a shower—but unfortunately no water. The proprietor was apologetic.

'No water until seven o'clock, señorita. But I shall make it especially for you!'

He fetched a spanner, unscrewed a few nuts, and after a while a trickle of luke-warm water dribbled down. When I went to switch on the light I found that there was no cover over the switch, only the bare wires. When I did manage to get it on it simply flickered feebly and then went off. This was soon put right by the proprietor, this time with a screwdriver.

With nightfall there was hardly a light in the whole town; obviously the lack of electricity was not confined to the hotel for even the *zocalo* was in darkness. In the market which was still active though lit only by oil lanterns, the ground was so full of holes and ruts that it was quite a perilous business picking one's way through. A candle burning inside a huge basket of fruit was sending out glowing ripples of colour through the plaited sides. Nearby a *petate* mat was spread with brown sugar animals, eggs and bananas, their owner, an elderly Indian, was fast asleep beside them. Ginger pottery shone in the candlelight with the intensity of a new horse-chestnut. Curious glances followed me, and once I heard the whisper—'*Está sola!*' ('She is alone!').

[94]

When I went to sleep that night between clean sheets the faint fragrance of bougainvillea drifted in through the door, which I had to leave wide open in order not to suffocate since there was no other means of ventilation.

Next morning the *zocalo* was clean and swept and ablaze with the orange flame of the poinciana. There was a continual procession with brown jars or kerosene tins to and from the stone well.

The heat was terrific and I was soon thankful to slip into the white church for a few minutes to get out of it. The floor was dusty and the benches worn and old, but the statues were elaborately dressed in robes of real silk; many had an armful of dusty pink paper roses trailing to the floor. One statue of the Child Jesus was the Spanish interpretation—an old-fashioned little figure in a long mantle and wide felt hat with turned-up brim and a feather. A large framed picture of the Virgin Mary had been opened, cheap earrings and a string of artificial pearls had been added, then the picture roughly put together again. There were so many artificial flowers that the few natural ones looked pale and uncomfortable.

In a glass case was a statue of a saint holding the handle of a wooden plough pulled by an ox and guided by an angel with cardboard wings. This was Saint Isidro who had been introduced by the Spaniards as the Patron Saint of Agriculture to take over from the God of Spring and Planting.

Back at the hotel I found a bus parked outside and the driver just emerging from underneath it; it had been there for half an hour with a breakdown and was leaving for Oaxaca in ten minutes. This was ideal; it just gave me time to pay the bill and collect my haversack.

Once we left Acatlán, cultivated fields of red earth began to give place to steep twisting roads which appeared to have been sliced out of the mountainside with a razor blade. Mountains lay in folds, deceptively like rose red silk, and the giant cacti that studded their valleys had seed pods that looked like tiny fluffy ginger kittens climbing up their stems.

It was nightfall before we reached Oaxaca. Not far from the bus station I found a small cheap hotel. This time there was not only a shower but also a strip of neon lighting and a bedside lamp —and they all worked. I was just preparing to enjoy all this luxury when the lights went out. Through the fanlight I could see that the rest of the hotel was also plunged in darkness. Obviously this was not a rare occurrence for, within minutes, I heard footsteps padding up the stairs and a lighted candle was placed outside my door. I took my shower by candlelight and then went out to explore Oaxaca.

The streets were narrow, and so dark that I wondered for a while, as I groped my way along, whether all the fuses in Oaxaca had gone. Apparently not, for suddenly I turned a corner and came into a veritable fairyland of light. It was the main *zocalo*. Magnificent Indian laurels, with trunks twisted into folds of silver-grey, encompassed it in a green benevolence; diamond-shaped beds of brilliant tropical flowers set down in vividly green coarse grass were placed geometrically around the bandstand. Light flooded out from cafés with tables set out on the pavement —something you rarely see in Mexico, though the weather seems perfect for it. Stalls were selling little figures of onyx, and the shining black pottery for which Oaxaca is famous, as well as colourful woven *zarapes*.

A *marimba* band now started up. The *marimba*, a gigantic xylophone of polished chestnut wood inlaid with black, was played by seven men in check shirts and straw hats, four on one side, three on the other. The rest of the band consisted of a double-bass, a drum and a tambourine. Shoeshine boys, ready to turn into *chicle* or popcorn sellers at a moment's notice, were everywhere; so were the equally persistent vendors of mysterious little paper packets containing hand-made filigree jewellery.

As the *zocalo* gradually filled up with the evening promenaders, men walking one way, women the other, I realized how vital a *zocalo* is in the life of a Mexican town or village where it is too hot to sit indoors in the evenings.

After three or four lively numbers, the perspiring players

downed their hammers and went off in search of a *refresco*. I went to examine the *marimba* more closely and found an inscription inside saying it had been constructed in Tuxtla Gutiérrez, Chiapas.

Next morning I decided to go as far as Tehuantepec. I would see more of Oaxaca on my way back, including the ruins of Monte Albán and Mitla.

I set my alarm for six o'clock and queued up for the front seat in a second-class bus. Ghost counterparts of yesterday's rose-coloured mountains loomed over the town as we rattled out of Oaxaca in a white mist. Ox carts driven by white-clad figures, their *zarapes* pulled tightly round them, were already on the road. Gradually there came an awareness of little towers of colour as hilltops of red earth pierced the mist.

As we wound up into the mountains, the driver, fresh to his day's work, drove so fast that it was like ascending and descending in a fast electric lift, but at a sideways angle. Once a truck with the inscription, 'God Will Save us', came hurtling towards us down a particularly precipitous incline. Both drivers, with a delighted scream of recognition, took both hands off their wheels to wave frantically at each other, just as we swerved past two wooden crosses on the roadside marking the spot where someone before us had gone hurtling over the precipice.

Like his friend, our driver apparently believed in the timely intervention of Providence, for, in addition to the vast number of holy pictures pinned to his windscreen, he also had a crucifix tied in front of the steering wheel, and was obviously of the opinion that with this host of the Unseen going ahead of him, he was relieved of all further responsibility. Accordingly we took all our hair-pin bends on two wheels, while far below us, turbulent rivers, caramel-coloured, swirled at the bottom of canyons where orchids hung like red lights against the dark rock.

Here in these central valleys of Oaxaca, among the peaks and pinnacles of the Sierra Madre del Sur, five thousand feet above sea level, the smallest pocket of soil is cultivated, for literally any-thing will grow in it from cabbages to pineapples, from marigolds to frangipani. It is here where the Sierra Madre del Sur suddenly breaks out into all these peaks, that it becomes two ranges instead of one. The rest of its course through the funnel-shaped land of Mexico is as the mighty Sierra Madre Occidental flanking the west coast, and the Sierra Madre Oriental, flanking the east.

From November to March not a drop of rain falls here so the valleys were still grey, yet already they were flickered through with the green of a few newly opened leaves, while here and there a solitary blossom—pink, orange or palest yellow—told of a real-life Sleeping Beauty who awaited, not even a kiss, but merely a few drops of rain, to awaken her.

Luckily the bus was not full so I was able to keep changing windows, for the view switched dramatically from one side of the road to the other as we climbed laboriously up one side of a range and then hurtled down the other. We accomplished this with such reckless speed and abandon that several passengers had turned quite green and were lying back with their eyes closed. I think I might have succumbed myself had it not been that the scenery was so magnificent that I could not bear to miss a moment of it. One had no sooner grown breathless at the beauty and majesty of one range, than another—even more majestic, even more beautiful—appeared ahead. (Or, from a more material viewpoint, just when one's stomach was thankful for a few moments on a flat stretch of road—*there* was another lot higher still! To anyone with a tendency to travel sickness I recommend a sedative pill before making this particular journey on a second-class bus.)

When we stopped for a meal we stepped out into a searing heat that nearly took my breath away. With the speed of the bus, the hot wind through the wide-open windows had merely seemed delicious. Outside it was like stepping into an open furnace. The 'restaurant' was merely a homestead of bamboo and thatch, with five or six old hammocks hanging under its sagging porch. Into these the passengers sank thankfully and lay there swinging and gasping in the heat. For myself I was glad enough to feel solid ground under my feet for a few moments and had no desire to go on rocking unnecessarily.

We reached Tehuantepec just at the hottest time of the day.

My bus, which had only stopped there for repairs, was going on to Tuxtla Gutiérrez in Chiapas—where the *marimba* had been made. It now occurred to me that once the Rainy Season started it might be neither so easy, nor so desirable, slithering round those hair-pin bends at that speed, and since, for all I knew there might be a great many more ahead, it might be as well to keep going while I could. Added to which a violent wind had transformed the streets of Tehuantepec into tunnels of hot dust so that I was not particularly impressed with it.

Accordingly, for a few *centavos* I bought a large green cocoanut at a market stall. The owner, one of the tall handsome women for whom Tehuantepec is famous, obligingly pierced the top with an old rusty skewer before thrusting a straw into it for me. Then I hurried back to where I had left the bus with its bonnet up and the driver head-first inside it. All was well. He was still there! I climbed on again, put my haversack back on the rack and began to suck eagerly at the cool, slightly sweet, cocoanut water which, after the dust outside, tasted like nectar.

The road out of Tehuantepec led past cocoanut plantations and swamps and some miles further on we had another 'meal stop'. (There seemed no time sense about these 'meal stops'. You simply ate because you had stopped and might not be given another chance to do so.)

This time there was a *'comida'* (dinner) for four *pesos*—soup, rice *'a là Mexicana'*, a plate of black 'beans of the pot', fruit paste and then hot chocolate.

High mountain ranges now barred our way into the jungle state of Chiapas, and soon we were climbing even more steeply than before between ever-deepening canyons. It was at this point that a khaki-clad official stepped out from nowhere and signalled us to stop. As we screeched to a standstill the hot air engulfed us like a wave. The official climbed on board and began to inspect the tickets. A foreigner? Where had I come from? Where was I going? Could he see my passport please? I realized suddenly that I had not thought of putting it in my pocket when I set off in the truck for Antonio's wedding. Now, apparently, we were heading for the Guatamalan border where a lot of smuggling had been going on. To add to this he had now discovered that I had originally booked to Tehuantepec . . . why then was I now going to Tuxtla Gutiérrez? The whole thing began to look extremely suspicious to him and he firmly refused to let the bus proceed as long as I was on it without a passport. In fact I must get off immediately!

It was the driver who saved the situation.

'It is true what the señorita says about Tehuantepec, officer,' he interrupted. 'I have not seen so much dust there myself for a long time. And if I put her off the bus in this wild place and in this great heat what can she do? She is alone.'

Finally, with a warning always to carry my passport in future, I was allowed to remain on the bus.

At Sante Fé we crossed into the State of Chiapas. And now, great as had been the mountains before, even mightier ones lay beyond; these in their turn fell behind while others still grander took their place. Once I caught a glimpse of an Indian on horse-back, his *zarape* flung over his shoulder, riding barebacked down a half-visible trail, pushing his way between vines laden with orange berries which hung down in ropes. I envied him passion-ately. To be an Indian, with an Indian's knowledge, riding alone through a State like Chiapas!

It was getting on for six o'clock before we reached Tuxtla Gutiérrez. I said goodbye to my nice driver, shouldered my haversack, and set off to find the *zocalo*—always my first point of exploration, as it usually meant the cleanest café in the town.

It was lively with music for there was a fiesta on. The market under the heavy trees was in full swing, and a large-scale game of *Lotería* (like Housey Housey) was taking place, with zinc pails and palm brooms as the prizes. But when I started looking for a hotel, I received a rueful shake of the head—'*Nada, señorita—nada. Es fiesta!*' I began to try the little side streets, but it was always the same. To add to this Tuxtla Gutiérrez abounded in mosquitoes—tiny ones that bit sharply and silently. My bare arms and legs were covered in them as fast as I brushed them off and everyone was

Cholula was full of elaborate churches
But the streets themselves were blank-faced and dusty

Mixteca Indians, hat-weavers. Guests at Antonio's wedding

'*Sombreros! Sombreros!*' By the roadside at Ixtapalapa on Good Friday

having the same trouble for there was a constant waving of hands and stamping of feet. I knew how to settle *that*! I walked into the nearest *farmácia* and asked for a bottle of mosquito repellent. The assistant shook her head. '*Nada, señorita—nada! Es fiesta!*'—and it was the same in every other *farmácia*. It looked as if I should have to sleep on a seat in the *zocalo* with the mosquitoes. My search had taken me round in a circle by this time and I found myself back in the side street where I had started. My bus still stood there, the driver squatting on his heels against the wall smoking.

'Hallo!' I exclaimed. 'Haven't you finished for today?'

He shook his head ruefully. 'They tell me now I must take this bus tonight to San Cristóbal de las Casas—two hours from here. And here is fiesta—and in San Cristóbal is no fiesta!'

I gave a despairing slap at the cloud of mosquitoes.

'Any mosquitoes there?' I asked.

'No, señorita—it is high in the mountains—more cold in the nights.'

No fiesta—so there might be a room! *And* no mosquitoes! I climbed back on to the bus again.

Gradually it filled up with passengers and mosquitoes in un-equal proportions but once we started and gathered speed the wind through the open windows soon disposed of the latter.

For a time Tuxtla Gutiérrez remained with us as pin points of light far below, but soon the immensity of the ranges swallowed us up again. It was a wild ride to San Cristóbal. Not only did we run straight into a thunderstorm, but the driver by this time had had just about enough of that bus and drove it through the dark-ness at an even fiercer speed than he had done by daylight, and over even more hazardous mountain roads because here they were not even made up in places. As we tore round these hair-pin bends, our wheels, spinning in the loose earth, pulled us right over towards the edge of the precipice. One passenger let out a shriek each time this happened, but luckily I was hardened to it after twelve hours, and so was able to enjoy the exhilaration of hot rushing darkness at the open window as tremendous sheets of lightning split the sky and zigzagged their way down into the dense jungle that fell away on all sides as we climbed up, seemingly into the very thunder which crashed and reverberated all round us. Once, in a dense valley far below, I saw, like a flickering line of fireflies, the pine torches of Zinacantecan Indians making their way home into the mountains.

It was ten o'clock before we finally came to rest with a shuddering gasp and a steaming radiator in one of the tiny streets of San Cristóbal de las Casas. Baskets and bundles were unloaded from the roof and the driver climbed down yawning, while I stood on the narrow pavement trying to decide in which direction to start my search for an hotel. He pointed down the street to a low plaster-washed house: 'Try first that *posada* (inn), señorita. It is small but clean. Very nice people.'

I pushed open the heavy wooden door and went in. Light from the kitchen was flooding out on to a tiny whitewashed patio filled with trailing maidenhair fern and carnations. The proprietor, a motherly lady dressed in black, had been busy slapping up *tortillas*, and came out wiping her hands followed by her daughter, black-eyed and beautiful, and also in black.

Yes, certainly she had a room! 'This way, señorita.' She opened a door off the patio into a room holding two beds covered with pink frilled bedspreads and heavy woven *zarapes*. The sloping wooden floor was highly polished; the tall window, protected by heavy iron bars, looked on to the street; and in one corner, behind a curtain, was a tiny tiled partition with a shower.

A meal?—she would get it ready at once! I came out after a shower to find a table laid for me in the tiny dining room looking on to the patio. Home-made soup was carried out by the first daughter, an omelette by a second daughter, as beautiful as the first, while a third, and smaller, followed with a bowl of rice and a large slice of papaya with two limes. While I ate, the three stood round me, smiling and encouraging me.

By contrast with Tuxtla Gutiérrez it was really cold here and I was glad of both *zarapes* on the bed that night. There was not a single mosquito; the only thing to disturb the peace were several large cockroaches which crept quietly up and down the wall all night and occasionally fell with a plop, upside down on their hard shiny backs, on to the floor.

In the morning though the sun shone from a cloudless sky the air was still crisp and cold, but by the time I had eaten my breakfast of sweet rolls and chocolate, served by one of the smiling sisters, it was already hot.

As soon as I saw San Cristóbal in daylight I knew I was going to like it. The narrow streets were lined with low plastered *adobe* houses in different colours (the clay had been mixed with pine needles instead of grass so that where the plaster had flaked off you saw little bristles sticking out) and there was that feeling of crisp cleanness that you usually get only by the sea. I remember those days in San Cristóbal as a small oasis of clarity and colour.

After breakfast I accompanied the eldest daughter to the market, the focal point for the Indians for miles around. It lay up a steep flight of steps which were crowded with Indians in their distinctive tribal costumes, their baskets and bundles piled up round them. There were gay good-looking Zinacantecans, their lean brown legs emerging from a creamy fringed shirt which reached just to the edge of very brief shorts; big tassels of puce-coloured wool swung from the ends of their woven scarves and a fall of mauve and pink ribbons dangled from the back of their wide flat hats. There were Chamula Indians with their cream woollen *zarapes* secured by a leather belt; their women, in a woven black garment to their knees, looked rather drab and timid.

Some Indians were carrying sacks of produce on their backs; others were driving a donkey weighed down on either side with enormous string nets filled with charcoal, pottery or the soft green *juncia* (pine needles) which are spread on pavements and floors for weddings.

In the maize market—an open space at the back—the shining heaps of grain were set out on *petate* mats. As a smiling Zinacantecan sitting cross-legged on the ground ladled out several quarts for her with a tin, the daughter from the *posada* explained to me that though the creamy maize is cheaper, the yellow is much finer and they always used it for their *tortillas*.

Afterwards she went from stall to stall buying her fruit, vegetables and herbs. Salt from the lagoons of Salina Cruz was piled up in great lumps on the ground; long strips of dried meat were sold in bundles, being more convenient for the Indians to cook on their open fires; small piles of what I mistook for oval sugar cakes turned out to be the lime for boiling up with the maize; larger quantities were being sold for whitewashing *adobe* houses. One man was selling vanilla, shaped into small brown sandcastles, for use instead of sugar; brown 'tulip bulbs' turned out to be *amol* which the Indians use instead of soap; alongside it were balls of black soap made of pigs' grease which froths up well when washing clothes in the river; there were also fragrant lumps of rosin for incense. A ragged Chamula woman squatting on the ground between the last two stalls was almost eclipsed under the white and gold trumpets of sheaves of arum lilies.

Unlike the markets in Mexico City, where the noise is often deafening, there was a peculiar undercurrent of silence here even though the market was thronged. The sellers just sat waiting quietly, for silence is a characteristic of the pure Indian. He seldom bothers with unnecessary conversation; even the children make very little noise.

In the main street of San Cristóbal the stores catered solely for the Indians, and little groups stood at the open doorways fingering the white fibre for making candles, the brown and red woven 'bits' and tailpieces for horses, and the coarse carrying nets. There were heavy pans for outdoor-cooking, waterproofed *zarapes* ready for the rainy season, and little oval wooden barrels for *chica* (an Indian drink made of maize) and for the fiery *aguardiente*, or Burning Water, made from fermented sugar-cane.

All the narrow streets led straight to the fields and foothills and I spent many hours wandering about there, for though the sunshine was intense it was never overpowering because of the crisp atmosphere.

I seldom saw anyone except a solitary figure working on a *milpa* (maize field) cut out of the hillside. One old man in faded blue cotton trousers, his brown face shaded by his old straw hat, was turning over the stubble with a hoe. He told me he did not own a plough but always 'ploughed' his *milpa* by hand. Oh yes, he said, it took him a long time—but then there was plenty of time! Further on a woman was washing clothes in the river where orange butterflies skimmed the water; I sat on a stone and watched the industrious yet unhurried way she rubbed the clothes on the stones, while her two tiny naked children paddled about happily, the hot sun glistening on their brown backs. After a while she sat back on her heels, smiled and pointed up the hillside to indicate where her village lay, but when I tried to speak to her in Spanish she shook her head. When she had finished she gathered up the clothes into a wide basket, placed it on her head, and set off with exquisite grace up the mountain track.

On the edge of the town lay the Indigenista Centre run by Dr. Villa Rojas and one afternoon I went along there hoping to see him and find out something of the work they are doing among the Indians. He was away in one of the villages but his assistant, Señor Dorres, was in his office. He took me round the orchards of pear and apple trees where two Chamula Indians in their short fringed *zarapes* were busy digging a new irrigation ditch; others were building a modern bungalow nearby. Half a dozen Indian girls with brightly coloured dresses, their dangling pigtails secured by a piece of ribbon or an elastic band, were being taught to play netball by a young Mexican, and were running about barefooted on a square of hot cement.

'We try to help them in three angles,' explained Señor Dorres—'education, agriculture and health. It is what you call Social Anthropology. Those Indians building the bungalow are Tzeltals.'

He led the way into a community room. 'Look, here is a list of some of the different languages of the Indians with whom we work in Chiapas—Zoque, Chol, Maya, Mame, Quiche, Chontal, Nahuatl.'

He was particularly proud of their puppet theatre.

'Through these we can teach them so much about health, agriculture and so on,' he explained. 'We have somebody here who speaks all their languages and the puppets are dressed up as things the Indians recognize—the Doctor, the Mosquito and so on. They hear the puppet talking their own dialect and can ask it questions and get answers back—and they love it! Come and meet our script writers.'

In a long low building four young Indians were busy on a new script—reading aloud and altering; another was busy painting a backcloth for the show, which is usually held out of doors.

'Here are the puppets themselves.' Señor Dorres pointed to a collection of wooden dolls, all collapsed legs and arms and pieces of string, only waiting for a voice and a hand to bring them to life.

'This is the Doctor—he has the face of Ignacio Barogan, the first head of this Centre! Here is the Barber, and this one represents *Agua* (water) which is so important to the Indians. These two sad ones are Sick Man and Sick Woman—and here are Happy Dog and Sad Dog! Through a dialogue between all these we are able to explain many things—how to avoid getting fever through bad water for instance.'

As we walked back to his office the two Chamulas were just finishing work—'And *I* shall be finished too in a few minutes,' said Señor Dorres. 'If you like we can have coffee together in the little café in the *zocalo*.'

We strolled into the town and sat in the window of the café.

'We had our fiesta here the other day,' he remarked, sipping his coffee. 'You should have seen the way the new Indians from the mountains took to the roundabouts! They didn't want to get off again! Everyone was promenading round and throwing confetti and I noticed one of our new Zinacantecans doing something with his feet. He was collecting up the confetti, and then walking along behind people and throwing it over them. *He* wanted to do what the others were doing! People ask them silly questions sometimes and they are very quick with their replies. Somebody once asked one of our Zinacantecans—"Don't you feel cold in your legs?" At once he replied, "Do *you* feel cold in your face?" They feel superior because they are pure Indian whereas most Mexicans are what they call "ladino"—a mixture of Spanish and Indian— *mestizo* we call it.'

As we left the café we met three of the Zinacantecans. They had merry laughing eyes and when introduced each shook hands with me four times. Then they asked Señor Dorres something in their own language. Laughing, he put his hand in his pocket, pulled out some *pesos* and handed them over and they went off gaily, striding across the *zocalo* on long brown legs.

Señor Dorres laughed. 'They work for us at the Centre—*such* nice fellows. They wanted to borrow some *pesos* till Saturday when they get paid! They are a very happy people—until they get drunk, then they start fighting. But usually they only drink with their own people.'

As we passed the open door of the big church two Chamula Indians were just going in. 'How do they get on in church?' I asked curiously.

'Well, it is now part of their life,' he answered. 'I would say the Indian goes to church to cry, to dance and to drink—and to speak to the saints! Come up to the Centre about ten o'clock tomorrow morning,' he added as we shook hands. 'Dr. Villa Rojas will be there and you can have a talk with him.'

I arrived next morning at one minute to ten to find a group of men standing outside the main office. Señor Dorres came hurrying over.

'I'm so glad you have arrived in time! That tall man talking to Dr. Villa Rojas is William Deneen from the States who arrived unexpectedly this morning. He is making a documentary film of Mexico for Encyclopaedia Britannica. Dr. Villa Rojas is just taking him to see our Centre for the Chanal Indians—you would have missed him if you had been one minute later! Come and meet him.'

I was introduced to Dr. Villa Rojas, a short dark virile man absolutely full of energy, and to tall William Deneen and his companion, fair-haired Bill Schindler.

'What about coming with us?' suggested Dr. Villa Rojas. 'I think you'd find it interesting. Mr. Deneen is taking his station wagon —you can come in my car.'

As we drove through the town Dr. Villa Rojas waved his hand frequently to acknowledge one of his Indians, or a woman with a baby tied to her back by means of her *rebozo*. At a turn-off in the foothills we started climbing up an earth road through pine forests followed closely by the station wagon. Waves of hot air coming through the open window were fragrant with fern and with rosin from the *ocote* tree, from which the Indians get their incense, and also their flares for walking through the mountains at night.

'Now we are right in the natural home of the Chanal Indian,' said Dr. Villa Rojas. 'It took us several years to build this road. The main thing we are trying to develop for them is transportation because they have to walk thirty or forty kilometres daily to take their produce to the market in San Cristóbal. We have put on a bus to take them there for only two *pesos* but even then some prefer to walk and save the two *pesos*!'

We came out on a high plateau overlooking deep valleys scattered here and there with huts.

The small low buildings of the Indigenista Clinic, surrounded by a white fence, consisted of a little consulting room, a tiny operating theatre, a room for the nurse who lives on the premises, a dormitory, with a stove in one corner and five or six trestle beds each spread with a *petate* mat, and finally a community room. All were spotlessly clean.

'For centuries,' explained Dr. Villa Rojas, 'this has been the crossing roads for the Indians on their way to the market at San Cristóbal. They must spend one night here. Before they just slept about in the open. Now they can sleep comfortably on a bed and start off early in the morning. We have a barber and a doctor and the nurse speaks their dialects and is able to translate for them.'

All the walls were painted in gay colours, and the ones in the little community room were covered in murals.

'Yes, aren't they good,' exclaimed Dr. Villa Rojas warmly; 'they were painted by our doctor! The buildings were made by the Indians themselves under supervision,' he went on. 'At first they thought our way of curing ailments was magical. Now many of the women even come to us from a distance to have their children, which shows a real degree of confidence. Altogether we have about eleven clinical centres.'

He told us that in their work they cover about ten thousand square miles and deal with over three thousand Indians.

'But they have always had a very well run society—better than ours in some way,' he said. 'The trouble is that for years they have been burning off the forests here for *milpas*—you can see the soil erosion that has resulted. We want to get them to cultivate things that will grow naturally up here, like Italian rye grass. We *have* managed to introduce fruit.' He pointed to a well-built wooden house surrounded by a ring of fruit trees.

Down in the valley, however, families were still living as in pre-Hispanic times. One woman, squatting on her heels on the ground weaving, had one end of her loom fastened to a post of the hut, the other attached to her waist exactly like the Aztec women on Rivera's mural.

'You see how flimsy the walls of the house are,' pointed out Dr. Villa Rojas. 'We are trying to teach them to build more solid houses because it is very cold up here at nights; we are also trying to stamp out typhus which came with the Spaniards. We want to organize them into a community so that they can have the benefit of medical supplies, water and agriculture. It would be much easier to give them these things if they were not so scattered.'

Inevitably one of us asked the question: 'Do you think they are happier for being civilized?'

'Well, if you have eight children it is more agreeable to have them alive than dead!' replied Dr. Villa Rojas drily. 'What we are trying to do is to organize them in a functional way according to modern times—but not to *over*-organize them. For instance, in Chicago nowadays nearly everybody uses tranquillizers. That is a completely artificial way of life—*that* is over-organization!'

William Deneen and Bill Schindler were now going out with

Señor Dorres to the village of Amatenango to see pottery-making.

'Why not come with us?' suggested William Deneen. 'There's plenty of room in the back.'

A steep earth track led up to the village of Amatenango—just a white church and a few long narrow earth streets with old wooden fences, but down every track there were breathtaking glimpses of mountain and jungle. Girls and women, pulling their *rebozos* across their faces, ran giggling to hide themselves behind the fences. A middle-aged woman, crouched on her heels in a yard, was just finishing making a water pot; her husband, in a torn khaki shirt, was stripping the threads from a *maguey* leaf.

'This village of Amatenango is the most important one for pottery-making among the Tzeltal Indians,' explained Señor Dorres, 'and it is always the wife who is the potter.'

Because it was a fiesta day here the younger women were in their best dresses—long dark blue skirts of heavy material just gathered together and held in place at the waist by a thick red sash; over this was a red jerkin with yellow stripes; round their necks they wore many gold chains and they had vermilion ribbons in their dark plaited hair. The old grandfather wore a khaki shirt; a red band round his waist held up his faded cotton trousers, and his hat had a long tassel hanging down behind; his shoes had high backs and sandal-like fronts. Their home was a windowless *adobe* hut with a palm roof.

Señor Dorres explained to the family, in Tzotzil, that William Deneen would like to photograph their pottery-making, and since they were quite willing the movie camera was set up, to the intense interest of several children who now appeared from the back of the hut where they had gone into hiding. They too wore thick red bands round their waists to keep up skirts of gathered blue material.

A wooden fence surrounded the little earth yard and in one corner was a tall avocado pear tree laden with fruit. Below, a wood fire was burning, and round it on pieces of board the finished pots were drying, each one being turned a little at intervals.

The wife now began a new one, first sifting some sand through a pot full of tiny holes, then taking a lump of clay and kneading the fine sand into it little by little. She made it in sections, using only her hands, and rolling out little strips which were always exactly the right length to go round; it was like laying little clay snakes one on top of the other and smoothing them in till you could see no join.

Presently four men came past carrying an old *marimba* on their shoulders, a poor relation of the fine one I had seen in Oaxaca. Rockets began to go up for the fiesta; in the sunshine they were nothing but a swish, a bang and a puff of smoke, but that was all that was required of them. The pot had now taken on a lovely rounded shape, and, after moulding the rim with a wet finger and fitting on little scraps of clay for handles, she placed it in the shade of the avocada pear tree to dry. The Tzeltal Indians do not use a kiln for baking, so later it would be put in front of the fire to bake. Meantime one of the others was ready for painting. In a hollowed-out stone she mixed some yellow powder and water and began to paint geometrical figures on the side of the pot.

Before we left Amatenango Señor Dorres took us to see the Indigenista Centre's clinic, which even had tiled showers. When we finally reached the outskirts of San Cristóbal I felt quite sorry the day had come to an end.

'Where are *you* going from here?' asked William Deneen as we drove through the *zocalo*.

'Well I haven't really thought about it yet,' I answered.

'We're driving across the Isthmus to Veracruz,' he said. 'I want to photograph the docks and the fishing there. Then we're going down to the coffee and banana plantations around Orizaba and back to Mexico City that way. Look—why not come with us? There's plenty of room in the station wagon. We'd enjoy having you. The only thing is we're leaving San Cristóbal right away—it doesn't give you much time to make up your mind!'

'I don't need it,' I said. 'It sounds perfect! I'll go right in and collect my things.'

I ran into the *posada*, said goodbye to the nice mother and daughters, and collected my haversack. A chance to go right across the Isthmus was too good to miss. Ten minutes later we were heading for the mountain road to Tuxtla Gutiérrez.

Before long we saw something zigzagging across the road in front of us. It turned out to be a young Zinacantecan Indian, about fifteen years old, and very drunk. The pink and mauve ribbons on his round flat hat dangled unhappily over one eye instead of down his neck, but *he* was far from unhappy, and was talking away animatedly to himself. We slowed down to walking pace, and as he saw the car he made a valiant attempt to get to the side of the road. Almost immediately he was back in the middle again; and each time we tried to pass him on either side he was there before we were, but gaily waving us on all the time.

'Heavens! It's worse than trying to get through a flock of sheep!' exclaimed William, and it was beginning to look as if this game of checkmate might go on indefinitely when there came a shout from behind. A group of older Zinacantecans, obviously relatives, came hurrying up, pulled our gay young friend to the side of the road, rating him soundly for his behaviour, while he continued to smile at us disarmingly and wave us on. The last we saw of him they were just picking him up for the third time as they frog-marched him homewards up a rough mountain track.

This time there was no fiesta in Tuxtla Gutiérrez and we found an hotel easily. The gardens were a multi-coloured bower of orange poinciana, pale blue plumbago and the scarlet star-shaped poinsettia—whose flower is not really scarlet at all but greenish-gold, and surrounded by long scarlet leaves. (In 1828 Joel Roberts Poinsett, U.S. Minister to Mexico, took such a fancy to it that he sent specimens to the States, where it was named after him, and later came to England as a greenhouse plant.)

Next morning we set out early for the Isthmus. It seemed strange, after queueing up for hours at bus stations in order to get a window seat, to find myself the occupant of the entire back of a station wagon with an unrivalled view on all sides.

Everywhere peaks tunnelled into the sky in a long and lovely sequence, and huge black butterflies flittered across the road as if someone somewhere was cutting up scraps of black chiffon.

This strip of approximately one hundred and ninety miles between Salina Cruz on the Pacific and Coatzacoalcos on the Gulf of Mexico is the narrowest part of the funnel-shaped Republic of Mexico. Varied projects have been put forward for making it into an alternative route to the Panama Canal. In the 1870's a Captain James Buchanan Eades wanted to build a ship railway so that ocean vessels from the Pacific could be pulled overland in special cradles and launched again on the other side in the Gulf, but the plan fell through.

The road across the Isthmus ran straight into the horizon for hour after hour between dry grassland. Once we came upon a dead cow lying in the middle of the road; on it perched a crowd of *zopilotes* (taken from the Aztec word, *tsopilotl*, and pronounced so exactly like 'Soppy Lottie' that I always thought of them as that). These huge black turkey vultures are the recognized Sanitary Inspectors of Mexico and they deal with all such matters quickly and efficiently, whether it be a large order such as this or a few scraps of garbage in a gutter.

Further north the scenery changed as we entered the rich State of Veracruz from which Mexico gets so many of her tropical products, among them sugar-cane, bananas, vanilla, rice and mahogany. Houses here were of widely spaced bamboo to let in the air. It was so hot now that you felt you could grasp the heat in handfuls. Sometimes a lorry with the tantalizing sign '*Tome* Coca-Cola' (Drink Coca-Cola) would come racing towards us; behind it, sizzling hot liquid bobbed about in bottles that looked ready to explode.

In the thick jungle-like vegetation of Veracruz are to be found deer, jaguar and wild turkey—the first live turkey seen in Europe was one which Cortés sent home from Mexico. He had found them in almost every Aztec household for it was the only creature which the Mexican Indian domesticated. So the turkey—along with poinsettia, chocolate, vanilla, tomato, dahlias, the rubber ball, and a great many other familiar things—is another of

Mexico's many contributions to the pleasures, culinary and aesthetic, of the Old World.

At Alvarado we queued up for the ferry behind a load of bullocks whose truck bore the inscription, 'I want to reach my destination'; the one behind, full of water-melons, declared, 'I trust in God'; while one on our right, loaded with hairy brown pigs, announced itself as, 'Rebel without Cause'.

The ferry, a dark lantern-lit bulk packed with lorries, cars and a couple of second-class buses, tried three times to make the landing; after a shouted consultation with those on shore it finally succeeded at the fourth attempt in getting alongside at the correct angle. When we were all jammed tightly on board, it pushed off into the darkness again, and after manœuvring about uncertainly for a while in mid-stream, got its bearings and headed for the opposite bank.

This was the great Papaloapan (Butterfly) River, whose banks at a certain time of the year are blotted out by thousands of butterflies just out of the chrysalis. Mexico seems to have a special attraction for butterflies for in the desert country of the north, the sky will at times be filled for twenty miles with butterflies migrating westward from the mountains to the sea.

Late in the evening we drove into Veracruz and found an hotel on the water front, which was lined with cocoanut palms. After a meal of 'red snapper a la Veracruzana' we went for a swim in water like warm silk which crept in over black sand, and where moonlight turned the thin breakers into threads of molten silver. After the heat and the long day's driving it was delicious. It was strange to be floating on those moonlit waters of the Gulf knowing that here on the 22nd April 1519, Cortés had landed (naming it 'The Town of the True Cross') to be met by Moctezuma's messengers bringing rich gifts of gold and jewels—all of which he graciously accepted before proceeding inland to overthrow the Aztec Empire. It was an amazing feat when you think of the handful of men he landed with—though I suppose one might say that the Aztecs had it coming to them sooner or later, since, by the Law of Cause and Effect, you cannot go on building up fear and hate around you indefinitely, as they were doing among the other tribes, without having it rebound eventually.

We spent the next day down on the docks. Dutch vessels were loading up with maize from the Central Plateau and a Spanish ship was taking on refined sugar. Car parts were being swung ashore—for Mexico has no car factories of her own but only assembly plants; bales of wool from Australia were being carried into the sheds; and a batch of new printing presses had just arrived. (The very first printing press in the New World was the one brought to Mexico City by the Spaniards in 1536, seventy-one years before the founding of the first English Colony in Jamestown, Virginia.) Shoe cleaners were doing a good trade re-polishing the shoes of Customs officials who had been inspecting sheds or ships.

Later, as we headed south leaving Veracruz and the Gulf behind, it grew hotter. Homesteads of thin wood with a palm thatch had deep overhanging porches under which all family activities were taking place. Hammocks would be swinging gently as a whole family took their siesta; a laden donkey would be tethered to a post while two men squatting down on their heels played cards on an upturned box; a young mother would sit rocking and sewing with a tiny naked brown baby crawling at her feet; a couple of schoolgirls in neat check uniforms would be doing their homework; or an old grandfather would be rocking gently back and forth in a cloud of tobacco smoke. Whatever the need, the porch was the answer to it.

As we neared Córdoba, the vegetation grew more lush and tropical. First came the mangoes—huge, shiny, dark-leafed trees with the round 'clipped' look of horse chestnuts, and giving a tremendous depth of shade; the oval yellow fruit on its long stems was fairly dripping from them. We began to pass homesteads with small sheds under which rows of thick brown tobacco leaves were hung up to dry; instead of orchards of mangoes, it was now mangoes plus a fragrant white sea of tobacco growing beneath them. Later they were joined by sugar-cane, sometimes lying in roughly cut bundles, then by bananas and coffee. Finally we reached the Grand Mixture—mangoes, tobacco, sugar-cane, coffee and bananas, all in one plantation.

Once we met a donkey wandering along the road; his load of feathery sugar-cane had half fallen off and was dragging awkwardly on the ground; far behind him trailed his owner, an elderly Indian, oblivious to everything except a single speckled lily which he was holding tenderly in his hand. By contrast we drove into Córdoba behind a truck in which sat three men with pistols. They were gesticulating so wildly that two of these were always pointing directly into our windscreen.

It was now dusk and we began to look for somewhere for the night.

'Hallo, that looks like an hotel!' exclaimed William in the little village of Fortin de las Flores. 'Let's try our luck.'

Yes, they could put us up quite easily.

'Well, I must say it looks nice—smells nice too,' remarked Bill as we passed through the lounge. Then, opening a door into the patio, we found ourselves faced with something so breathtakingly beautiful that we all stopped dead.

It was a swimming pool—but what a swimming pool! Its lime-green water was softly floodlit, the whole surface luminous with thousands of white gardenias floating face upwards, giving out an intoxicating fragrance. It lay in isolated beauty half enclosed by the pillared patio and half by tropical gardens where spotlights picked out single jewel-like sprays of scarlet bougainvillea, of orange poinciana, or pale-blue plumbago out of which tall umbrella palms rose like shadows into a star-studded sky. All these only intensified a hundred times the ivory whiteness of that carpet of blossom.

I shall never forget the hour that followed. As I climbed down into the warm soft green water, the gardenias closed around me instantly, like some white cloak that fastened at the chin and then floated up and out into space. As I began to swim flowers moved stiffly against my face and shoulders, yet their centres were soft as silk. As for the fragrance—think of one gardenia then multiply it by two thousand!

The family of the potter in the village of Amatenango, Chiapas

Tzeltal woman potter at work, Amatenango

Wood for guitars drying in the sun in the village of Paracho

Guitar maker in the village of Paracho

The Pool of Gardenias

'Well, I *said* something smelt nice!' remarked Bill as we climbed out reluctantly at last.

After dinner we sat in long cane chairs on the patio. By that time the moon had risen, and now, beyond the shadowy palms and the scarlet bougainvillea, far away on the indigo horizon like an echo of the dazzling whiteness at our feet, was etched the snow-clad peak of Mount Orizaba, Mexico's highest volcano, 18,850 feet high.

Late that night two gardeners in straw hats began to take the gardenias out of the pool, heaping them along the edge of the patio. I took off my sandals and waded ankle deep in the soft wet coolness before they were carried off to be spread as fertilizer on the coffee and banana plantations. About two thousand gardenias are picked early each morning in the fields and plantations around Fortin and brought here in truckloads.

I got up early to watch the fresh ones being carried in in great baskets and tipped out into the pool till the green water was once more a scented froth of white.

At lunchtime a Mexican wedding party arrived bringing with them a group of musicians and two dancers. They performed all the typical Veracruz dances—the girl in high-heeled red shoes, swirling skirt and lace shawl dancing between the tables while the guests clapped in rhythm.

It was typically Mexican dancing for pure Indian dancers always had bare feet, sandals or low deerskin shoes; the Spanish introduced high heels and the wide skirt. The *rebozo*, which both Indian and Mexican women wear, was also introduced by the Spaniards so that the Indian women should have something over their heads in church.

Before leaving Fortin we spent several hours in the plantations wandering between aisles of bananas, their inner leaves vividly green, the thick outer ones split into stripes as if with scissors. Bushes of coffee in between were covered in tiny white flowers; some already had little oval green berries turning red.

Late that afternoon we began to head back for Mexico City across plains where ripening barley was fenced by huge *nopal* cacti, their round discs ringed with rose-red blossoms; somehow barley and cactus (especially cactus in blossom) struck me as being the most incongruous partnership anyone could have dreamt up.

'Well, there they are!' exclaimed William as late that night we rounded a bend and saw the lights of Mexico City spread out in the valley.

'It's been awfully nice having you with us,' he added. 'We'll be doing some filming in another part of the country, probably the centre, later on. Would you like to come?'

'I'd love it!' I exclaimed.

'Right,' he said. 'I'll let you know when it is and we'll pick you up. And now we'll drop you right on your doorstep—if you tell us where it is!'

And so, with William and Bill waving from the window, the station wagon vanished into the darkness, leaving me standing once more in front of the familiar wrought-iron gate at San Angel. I had travelled over one thousand two hundred miles since I climbed into that truck armed with the wedding dress!

CHAPTER 9

PAPANTLA AND THE VANILLA GODDESS

ONE MORNING I set off to find my way to Papantla, the country of the Totonac Indians which lay somewhere in the State of Veracruz; I wanted to see the ruins of the great seven-storey Pyramid of El Tajín which Diego Rivera has portrayed so magnificently on one of his murals at the National Palace. There was no bus to Papantla itself but I found one going to Pachuca, which was in the right direction.

Great hills surrounded this little silver mining town, and women and donkeys were toiling up and down the narrow alleys with water jars. My explorations there that evening led me into the courtyard of a school which was used at night for adults as well as for children. An old man, sweeping up with a palm-leaf brush, told me proudly that they had a teacher who spoke English. 'I will take you to see him,' he said. 'He will be very pleased.'

He crossed the courtyard and pushed open a shabby door to reveal a crowded classroom. Plaster was peeling off the walls in great chunks and the children were barefooted and very grubby; four or five adults were seated awkwardly at the small desks.

The young teacher shook hands with me. 'I love to speak English,' he said, 'but I seldom have the opportunity. I study much by myself after school. Will you stay and hear our lesson, señorita? You can sit at my desk. It is a lesson on hygiene.' He glanced a little sadly round his class. 'I am afraid it is much needed.'

He began to hold up painted banners depicting different scenes. The first showed a man in bed; his eyes were closed and one bare brown arm lay outside the bedclothes; a large and aggressive-looking mosquito was about to dive upon this. Underneath was the wording in Spanish, 'This is a mosquito that gives *paludismo* (malaria).'

The next, which brought a shriek of delight from all the small boys, showed a skull and crossbones; the wording told us that two million persons in the world die every year from *paludismo*.

Next there was a man holding a spray, and surrounded by mosquitoes. 'What must he do?' enquired the teacher hopefully.

'Fleet!' (Flit!) shouted the class as one; this he corrected to '*Insecticida*', and then went on to show us a man spraying petrol on a swamp. This was the end of the lesson.

'It has been a pleasure for me to be speaking to someone from England,' he said as he shook hands with me.

As the bus headed eastwards next day, valleys rich with ferns began to fall away on either side of the road. Sometimes we would pass an Indian with the load of wood on his back secured by a woven band round his forehead. Whenever I saw the Indians carrying heavy burdens in this manner I thought of the Aztec bearers who, carrying their burdens in exactly the same way, had run miles in a sort of relay race passing on from one to another fresh foods from all parts of the Aztec Empire for the table of the Emperor Moctezuma in his Palace at Tenochtitlan.

As we neared Poza Rica the landscape became dotted with thin bright spears of flame—the outlet from the oil fields. Outside a large depôt announcing 'Petroleos Mexicanos—At the Service of the Country', the soldier on duty was sitting on the pavement with his arm round a girl selling pumpkin seeds.

Early next morning I was on my way to Papantla. An old Indian woman with her tiny grandson came and sat beside me. She told me they had been travelling for two days and were returning to their village in the mountains. I took the little boy on my knee so that he could look out of the window and he quickly lost his first shyness. His black eyes lit up with excitement as we passed the leaping gold torches in the undergrowth, but after a while his lashes began to droop, and soon he fell asleep. His grandmother took him then, and they both slept, she with one gnarled brown hand protectively over his eyes.

The bus now began to thread its way through hot jungle country. In one of the deep engulfing valleys lay the little town of Papantla, its tiny coloured houses in tiers up the hillside. The *zocalo* with its tiled seats was over-laced by gigantic Indian laurels and being Saturday it was thronged with Totonac Indians who had come in from the surrounding villages. Next day happened to be Palm Sunday—something I had not realized—so there were extra crowds for that is a special fiesta in Papantla.

The Totonac men wore baggy snow-white cotton pantaloons tied tightly round the ankles with tapes; a short white shirt gathered into tucks on a yoke at the back, fell loosely to the waist; a small coloured handkerchief rolled into a strip was knotted round the neck; their big white hats had huge upturned brims, and they all carried a hemp bag over one shoulder. Below the white pantaloons emerged bare dusty brown feet, or, very occasionally, riding shoes and bare ankles, but these merely looked incongruous whereas the brown feet looked absolutely right.

The women had white dresses to their ankles, the shoulders sometimes crocheted in colour; a bib of rose, orange or lime-green chiffon was secured round the neck and tucked in at the waist above an apron of different coloured silk; their black plaits were looped back by a coloured bow, and round their shoulders they wore white embroidered lace shawls. Whereas the men's dusty brown feet looked quite natural below the snow-white pantaloons, somehow it looked all wrong to see dusty brown feet protruding below these lovely embroidered dresses.

The men had thin serious brown faces and high cheekbones. Many had come in alone and they sat on the tiled seats in an attitude of absolute quiet, their hands folded in their laps as if in meditation; by comparison with some who obviously considered themselves superior and emancipated in modern check shirts and slacks, they had an air of detached serenity that was noticeable and enviable.

The women, who seemed less mature, gathered in little groups, laughing and giggling; they kept their money in handkerchiefs thrust down their coloured bibs and were continually taking it out to count it.

In the market, a labyrinth of dark uneven passages closely packed with stalls, coloured bibs, aprons and crocheted shoulders for dresses hung among the pottery, fruit and vegetables. Most of the stalls were selling little tins containing sticky dark-brown vanilla beans twisted into shapes of baskets, animals or flowers; their aromatic scent pervaded the whole market.

The finest vanilla in the world is grown in these rich valleys, of which Papantla is the centre, for this hot jungle country is the home of the vine which bears the tiny ivory-white orchid that develops into the heavily scented vanilla bean. Thousands of Totonac families depend on it for their living, and long before the Spaniards came the Totonac Indians were growing vanilla around Papantla and paying the beans as part of their tribute to the Aztec Emperor.

For centuries the vine grew wild in these jungles, but now it is cultivated you rarely find it growing wild. To make a new field the Indians take their *machete* knives and clear about three acres of jungle, leaving just young saplings that will give a good shade. Then for two years they raise crops of corn on the plot and on the third year plant one or two slips of vanilla vine and tie them to the trees. Like the *maguey*, the vanilla is a long-term policy for it does not flower until its sixth year, but then goes on flowering until about the twelfth.

When ripe for picking, the pod is rather like a runner bean, but inside are thousands of tiny black seeds in a sticky sap which is the source of the vanilla essence. When the bean has gone through its long curing process to reduce the moisture it is dark brown and sticky. It keeps its fragrance for a long time and the little baskets and animals of beans are put among clothes to scent them.

In Mexico vanilla has always been considered sacred to the Totonacs. The legend says that when the gods were still on earth, Xanat, the lovely daughter of the Fertility Goddess, fell in love with a Totonac boy. As she could never marry him she turned herself into the flower of the vanilla vine so that she would always belong to the Totonac boy by belonging to his people—and even today the Totonac Indian calls the flower of the vanilla, Xanat. It is curious that it was only found growing around the country of the Totonacs and was unknown to the rest of the world till Cortés sent the beans home to Spain; it was the Spaniards who christened it 'vanilla', or 'little sheath'.

However, when they tried to grow it elsewhere it would not bear fruit. The Belgian botanist, Charles Morran, discovered that pollination could only be effected by a certain tiny honey-bee that only frequented the Totonac district. By inventing a method of artificial pollination he became the first man to produce vanilla pods outside Mexico. Madagascar now produces most of the world's vanilla, but by artificial pollination. The Totonacs still produce ninety-eight per cent of Mexico's vanilla and connoisseurs claim that the best vanilla still comes from around Papantla.

Being fiesta day it was also Visiting Day at the jail, and a constant stream of women went up and down the steps carrying baskets of *tortillas*, and blue zinc pans of cooked food, which were inspected by the guard to make sure they contained no weapons or fire-crackers.

'How many prisoners have you got?' I asked.

'About seventy,' he replied, 'but many are without a visitor—if you like you can visit one, señorita.'

I joined the queue into the dark room, one end of which was divided off by iron bars; through a square hole in the centre the visitors were pushing their baskets and pans while the prisoners seized their gifts. One of the 'visitorless' prisoners, a swarthy young man, came close to the bars so that we could carry on a conversation above the bedlam. After a little polite conversation I asked him—not quite sure how to put it tactfully—what he was 'in' for. He was evasive . . . nothing really . . . there had been an accident . . . someone had died. When I asked the guard afterwards he made a gesture of cutting someone's throat and sticking a knife in their ribs and shrugged as if to say, 'You know the sort of thing.'

As the shadows lengthened people began promenading round

the *zocalo*, men one way, women the other, children in the centre. As the snow-white costumes, the bright colours and the soft tread of bare feet mingled under the deepening gold of the lanterns in the trees, I felt the completeness of this little *zocalo*, a focal point of light in the heart of the jungle-clad valleys that surrounded it.

I managed to get a room for the night, and early next morning heard the sound of a drum and saw a small procession coming down the street in a swirl of colour. It was the dancers on their way to start the fiesta. I joined the small crowd behind them and we made our way up a flight of steps to a courtyard in front of the church.

As with most pure Indian dancing the music was simply a wooden flute with a high sweet plaintive note, and a drum, but together the two managed to work themselves, and the dancers, into a fine frenzy.

The leader of the dancers wore a helmet-shaped head-dress and held a hobby horse in front of him; his red silk cloak had a gold fringe, and there were gold fringes round his ankles. The others, also in red silk costumes, had head-dresses studded with tiny mirrors and decorated with streamers; each carried his *machete* knife which, in the ordinary way, he used for clearing the jungle for his vanilla planting.

The church was the backcloth—a dark yawning cave compared to the brilliance outside, though flickered at the far end by candle-light. A constant stream of white-clad figures came up and down the flight of stone steps, where bundles of thin palms decorated with coloured paper were for sale. Soon every woman carried one, so that the audience, now swelled into hundreds, was like a bed of unusual flowers—white stemmed, brown faced and spiralled with colour.

Faces of both dancers and audience were serious and intent. Apart from the high notes of the flute and the sonorous beat of the drum, the only sound was the tinkling of a cluster of little bells which the leader carried, and with which, combined with shouts, he directed the dancers like a 'caller' at a square dance. Each one in turn advanced into the centre to clash their gleaming *machete* knives with him and then with each other. Then, cloaks swirling, they spun round and round drawing the points of their knives in a circle on the ground with a rasping sound, sending the dust flying up in our faces.

When at last they ceased, dripping with perspiration, their silk garments clinging in dark patches to their backs, there was no applause, and after a brief rest they simply began all over again.

As their ancient Vanilla Festivals coincide with various Church festivals the Totonacs combine the two by doing the dances outside the church door. At Corpus Christi they perform the Flying Dance, in which four men, dressed as birds and representing the four seasons, climb to the top of a dizzily high pole where a fifth man is seated on a tiny wooden platform playing a drum. Each dancer is tied by one foot to a separate rope wound round the pole, and at a given signal the four dive head-first into space, playing their flutes as they whirl round and round upside down thirteen times, equivalent to the fifty-two year cycle. This causes the platform, where the fifth man is doing a dance, to revolve.

The church was now filling up with families waiting for their palms to be blessed. When finally a priest did appear at the altar the dancers were forgotten and figures began running up the aisles on bare feet till the front of the church became an agitated sea of colour; a few minutes later the aisles turned into moving coloured processions as white figures returned triumphantly with their blessed palms which were decorated with anything from coloured paper to straw stars, gladiolis, a bunch of weeds, or even a flowering onion head. A man with an eye to business had stationed himself outside the door with hair ribbons, holding them up like a coloured curtain, and picking out unerringly the right colour to match each bib as it approached.

The dancers went on unweariedly all afternoon, but this time in the *zocalo* under the shade of the laurels—always the same dance and always surrounded by an admiring but silent audience.

Once, in the midst of the festivities, an open lorry drew up opposite full of helmeted soldiers with rifles at the ready. In the midst of them, hatless, their shirts torn open, were two men, tied to the nearest soldiers by ropes. With a battery of rifles pointed at them they were marched into the police station to add to the seventy already behind bars; neither dancers nor audience took the slightest notice of this interruption.

Meantime I went to find the ruins of El Tajín which lay several miles distant from Papantla. A little bus passed near the turn-off and once there I made my way up an earth track between dense vegetation. Suddenly, rounding a bend, I found myself face to face with an enormous ruin. Seven storeys high, it stood in grey and solemn grandeur against a background of thick jungle; even with the great stairway half collapsed, and the top storey crumbled away into a faint reflection of its former glory, I recognized the great Pyramid of El Tajín.

What I had taken on the mural for windows, I now discovered to be the remains of three hundred and sixty-five blind niches which had once held a statue of a god for every day of the Totonac's 365-day Calendar. The staircase was still partly decorated with hieroglyphics; piles of great carved stones showing Totonac priests in ritual postures lay about in the undergrowth.

An elderly Totonac sitting on a heap of stones told me that at this Pyramid of El Tajín, or Thunder, his people had worshipped the Wife of the Sun God, the Goddess Ceneutl—'Lady surrounded by Divinity'. They had also called her 'The one who takes care of the products of the land that you eat', and had loved her very much because she did not want human sacrifice, only offerings of birds and fruits from the hills. They had offered these to her in the temple which had once stood on top of this Pyramid. The Totonacs believed she was the one who intervened for them with the Great God, and that one day she would send another Sun to free them from the Aztecs, of whom they were very much afraid because of their continual demand for human sacrifice, which the Totonacs thought dreadful.

A track led up a small hill nearby and I began to climb this in order to look down upon the Pyramid. The further it receded the more beautiful it became as, framed by the fingers of branches, it settled deeper and deeper into its surroundings of jungle.

Over the hilltop I found other ruins, the palaces of this great ceremonial centre, and numberless mounds hiding others not yet excavated, but there was nothing to touch the Great Pyramid for sheer beauty. By the time I looked down upon it again the sun was setting in a great aura of colour that merged sky and ruin into one tender radiance of rose.

I stayed on, loth to leave as long as the stones were still gilded by the sunset. Here in Mexico, where the ruins of a decayed greatness everywhere impinge upon the consciousness of the present, the veil that divides the living from the dead is very thin —and never more so than at El Tajín. Here, indeed, in Shelley's words they seem to 'move like winds of light on dark and stormy air'.

As I walked back down the earth track I met a family of Totonacs on their way to the Pyramid. The man, with his thin grave face, strode ahead; the woman followed, her decorated palm in her hand, a brown baby astride her hip. Even so must their ancestors have come on just such an evening when the vanilla beans were at the climax of perfection, to give thanks to the Goddess Ceneutl. All the way back to Papantla I passed such families on their way home; they would turn off down small tracks to be lost within seconds among dense vegetation.

Next morning I found a bus that was going to San Raphael; from there I could get a connection to Mexico City. But, added the driver, as an after-thought, he was going a very roundabout way by the Gulf of Mexico—it would take many hours. That suited me perfectly. Half my pleasure on such a journey comes from not knowing exactly where I am going or when I am going to get there.

Immediately we started, the driver switched on his portable wireless and we drove along in the torrent of sound—ninety-nine per cent atmospherics and one per cent so-called 'music'—that is typical of Mexican buses and cafés. Outside, feather-white morning mist shrouded the silent valleys and the broad-leaved banana plants were dulled as if breathed upon. One day, I thought, a generation of Mexicans, brought up in this incessant barrage of noise, may well find themselves paying to 'listen' to such a silence.

At Tecolutla the bus ran on to an old ferry and we zigzagged our way in brilliant sunshine across a wide river lined with cocoa-nut palms. Then, for an hour or more, we drove alongside the Gulf of Mexico—on one side the wide empty beach sparkling with long glass-green rollers, on the other cocoanut and banana plantations. There was no trace now of that early morning mist; the world was glittering in sunshine and temperatures had soared up into the nineties. To me, on such a Mexican morning of hot sun out in the country, a second-class bus—even as old as this one which broke down several times before we reached San Raphael —was infinitely preferable, with its wide-open windows, to any First Class bus with sealed windows and air conditioning.

Young banana plants, only ankle high, were of such a trans-parent green that they had a strangely 'defenceless' look. Some-times they were 'protected' by a wall of tall feathery maize, and this soon developed into a Mutual Benefit Society for, further on, fields of equally young maize would be surrounded by a 'fence' of brown-trunked adult banana plants, their sheath-like red flowers hanging down like a spiral. Sometimes orange trees, their tiny white blossoms filling the whole bus with overpowering sweet-ness, would be planted between the bananas; at other times maize, bananas and oranges would be knit together in one dense wall of green.

Homesteads were only thin huts, but each was turned into a bower of blossom—by mauve bougainvillea, creamy frangipani and orange poinciana. In the coffee plantations the beans had been stripped off leaving thin spidery branches sticking out. As we climbed up into mountain ranges split by great gullies, down which ferns, twenty feet high, cascaded like water, incredible vistas opened up on every side. As on so many occasions I found the right-hand side of the bus got the best views.

The driver would frequently take out an old tin and fill it with water in some village to top up his steaming radiator. At one tiny bus station he stopped to remove two roses which were wilting in a rusty vase below the picture of the Virgin of Guadalupe and came back with a stem of pink gladioli which he placed lovingly in position; a little while later he stopped at a roadside shrine to jump out and light a candle.

It was evening before I found myself heading towards the Central Plateau again. Flimsy huts had given place to solid structures of thick board or stone and Indians were carrying folded *zarapes* over their shoulders, a sure sign that nights and morning were cold. The bus was besieged the instant it stopped by women with baskets of sweets, the speciality of that particular town. Once it was crystallized fruits—whole halves of orange skins, melon or pineapple; another time lumps of candied 'barrel' cactus. If a bus going in the opposite direction pulled up at the same time the sellers became nearly frantic rushing from one side of the road to the other.

Soon we were back in the land of grey *adobe* huts, of vast plains powdered yellow with old maize stalks, of serried ranks of grey-green *maguey*, of ruined *haciendas*, and of dried-up lake beds. Long before we reached Mexico City we ran into a thick dust storm in which the road completely disappeared before and behind, while church domes and telegraph poles came and went in a cloud as if materializing and dematerializing.

CHAPTER 10

GOOD FRIDAY AT IXTAPALAPA

ON GOOD FRIDAY I was up early to get a bus to Ixtapalapa where every year the inhabitants put on their own Passion Play.

'Always at three o'clock a hot wind gets up and the sky loses its blue,' Margarita had said the night before. However, the sky had never looked a more perfect blue, so this year was obviously going to be an exception.

At every stop people clambered on to the bus clutching baskets, bundles and *petate* mats.

In the suburb of Ixtapalapa straw hats—big ones, small ones, all shapes and sizes—were piled up on the pavements or in the hollows on dusty earth banks. '*Sombreros, sombreros!*' shouted a tiny boy in front of me delightedly, banging his small fists on the bus windows.

It was still only eight o'clock but already the large earth square of the market had an air of activity. Corn cobs, looking like creamy lilies, were being thrown into huge rusty cauldrons to boil; *nopal* cactus were being cut up and boiled for a special Easter dish with fish and eggs. Some stall-owners already had huge brown *cazuelas* of this cooking.

When I asked a policeman what time the procession was due he said ten o'clock. Allowing for Mexican time I judged that to mean midday; in fact it turned out to be one o'clock.

On either side of a steep earth track leading off to the right were more stalls, and many charcoal *braseros* for cooking *tortillas*. Sacks of oranges were being emptied on to the ground; papaya and melons were being cut down into slices so that they looked like huge flowers; and great blocks of ice were being dragged up the dusty track on the end of a rope.

These beginnings of a fiesta day gradually became wider apart till by the time I got well up the track there was only an odd stall or two. Yet still it led upwards between dusty ridged fields and pepper trees, and always there were one or two toiling figures ahead of me, most of them laden with pails and baskets, intent on some unseen destination. Then as we rounded a bend, I saw what we were all toiling towards. On the hilltop two rough wooden crosses stood out against the sky; between them was reared a single post. Here was the Calvary.

The women with their baskets merged into the shade of tree or rock and settled down to wait. The roofs and domes of Ixtapalapa lay far below me now, the rough hillside between us empty and silent. It could have been *any* dry hillside split by canyons of soil erosion, feathered sparsely by the pale green of pepper trees—I had seen many such in the Valley of Mexico—but because of those three silhouettes against the sky it was different. It was a hillside charged with expectancy . . . brittle with waiting.

More figures began to appear, antlike on the dusty track up which I had come; mostly they were family groups carrying between them a pail of water, baskets of food and a couple of *petate* mats. More stalls began to appear by the wayside; the first *tortillas* were being slapped into shape. Little blue zinc basins of chile and raw onion, of tomato and sliced *nopal* cactus, were being prepared for *tacos*—but no meat as it was Good Friday.

A Red Cross tent had been erected half-way up the hillside; it held two stretchers and blankets. Four or five eager young men in khaki and four young girls in white aprons told me with delight that there would be *mucha gente* (many people) and—they hoped—many casualties to allow them to demonstrate their efficiency. At this moment there came a shout from the road far down in the valley. A car accident! Within seconds the four young men had seized the two stretchers and were running, leaping, down the rough hillside.

'But surely they won't bring them right up here?' I exclaimed to one of the girls.

'Oh *yes*!' she said emphatically, and her eyes shone as she began to tip the entire contents of the First Aid box on to the floor in anticipation.

Down below, the crowds in the streets and the square had swelled into thousands. On *refresco* stalls huge glass containers of fruit juices glistened in the sun—the pale green of lime, the fawn of the *tamarinda* bean, the rich red of water-melon juice thickly sprinkled with black seeds, the pale orange of papaya juice. One man was adding so much water to his jars from a rusty kerosene tin that new customers were soon getting only an apology for the original. When only a small quantity of water remained in the tin he carefully tipped some out into his hands, washed his hair with it, shook the last drops over the wheels of his wooden cart and trundled off with the tin to refill it at the well in the cemetery where there was a long queue with pails, jars and tins.

Suddenly there was a stir and a splash of colour. The crowd scattered to right and left as a Roman centurion, herald of the coming procession, came galloping through the square, his helmet glittering, his red cloak flying out behind him. Following him on foot came a small group, wending their way slowly towards us. It was Mary and the women. In that world of smooth plaits, their long black hair hanging loosely down their coloured mantles did more than anything to lend an air of unreality to the scene. They walked quietly, not looking to right or left, their bare brown feet noiseless on the dusty earth road.

At the same moment I noticed another small group, but this one was making its way with difficulty in the opposite direction against the crowd. First came a man carrying an enormous mauve and silver wreath which he held up like a banner; behind him came four men bearing on their shoulders a slender coffin. A small group of mourners followed, the women barefooted and all in black, their limp black cotton *rebozos* held across their faces.

The Centurion reined his spirited horse for a second, and

The Pyramid of El Tajín near Papantla, State of Veracruz

Totonac Indians on their way to the Pyramid

Margarita Urueta in the library, beneath her portrait by Siqueros

The author beside a *nopal* cactus, Central Mexico

acknowledged the coffin with a swift but reverent movement of his head. For a moment the two little groups of mourners—so different, yet so akin, since both were concerned with the transition which we call 'death'—were level with each other. Then they had passed—the one to make its way to the cemetery, the other to the hilltop.

By now thousands of spectators lined the square and the track up that hillside. The sun beat down fiercely and a small wind which had sprung up swirled the dust into our faces as we stood packed tightly together, scarcely able to breathe. Four or five horses, their heads decorated with tassels, were ridden by young men whose duty it was to keep a way clear for the coming Procession. This they did by backing their horses firmly into the crowd, jamming us still tighter together.

Now came a fanfare, and four gold-clad trumpeters appeared, their horses rearing up uneasily at the sound and at the terrific pressure of people hemming them in. Following them, amid a waving of coloured pennants, came a whole contingent of Roman soldiers, their cloaks colourful, their helmets glistening.

Then came Pilate riding alone, and after him, dragging their crosses, the two thieves, one—a huge white-haired man with wild eyes—naked except for a loin cloth. They passed on between the now silent crowd while behind them, alone, bowed beneath the weight of a great cross, came the Christ. Below the white robe were bare brown feet; on the head with its smooth flowing hair was a crown of real thorns.

At the sight of him the crowd surged forward. Many tried to touch him, crying out 'Christus! Christus!' They were forced back by a chain of young men who, with linked arms, formed a living barrier that moved along with him. Some distance behind, like an echo and an escort, came two rows of young men, each dressed in a simple mauve garment, each wearing a crown of white thorns, each bent under a smaller cross. Lastly came Mary and the women with downcast heads.

As soon as the procession had passed there was a rush by those in the square to get to the hilltop ahead of it. There was no question of being able to go up alongside the track; it was already packed hundreds deep on either side. All we could do was to go by way of the hillside, and the dust rose in clouds as scores of pounding feet began to break up the dry clods.

Whenever we came to a steep gully we spread out like ants, in all directions, stumbling in and out of the dust-filled hollows. It was a crowd out for the day to see a crucifixion—only this time with sympathy not condemnation. Of course there were those who were indifferent, now as then—laughing groups who sat about in the meagre shade of the pepper trees, sinking their teeth thirstily into soft orange slices of papaya, or dipping their rolled-up *tortillas* into little brown bowls of hot chile sauce bought in the market—for there will always be those who are content to sit back while the great drama of life, material and spiritual, is enacted around them. But there was an urgency and a unity among the rest of us as we scrambled and jostled our way up the hillside in the swirling dust.

When we reached the top, however, we found the crowd to be even greater than that below. Figures were perched up on the branches of every gnarled pepper tree, and all that we could see was a cloud of dust advancing between the packed rank of watchers. In it, dimly, we could make out the pikes with their coloured pennants and the glitter of a helmet—that and the tip of a cross that moved slowly and unsteadily, pausing for longer and longer intervals.

I realized suddenly that the sky, which had been so blue, was now the colour of steel and that the little breeze of an hour or so earlier had become a strange hot wind. I looked at my watch. It was a quarter to three.

Just then a sudden shift in the crowd in front enabled me to get a footing on a small boulder. At the same moment the tip of the cross drew level with me and I was able to see the white-robed figure below it. The robe was covered in dust now from many falls and the smooth hair was damp and tangled. His bare feet had been cut by the sharp flinty track and he was walking slowly and painfully, while the weight of the crown had driven some of the thorns into the forehead so that a trickle of blood mingled with the perspiration that was pouring down his face.

There was a sea of heads between us, yet, for one instant, as he paused to shift the weight of the cross upon his bowed shoulders, his eyes met mine.

Two thousand years telescoped into insignificance . . . Mexico and Jerusalem merged into one.

A few moments later and the multitude of thousands upon that hillside was looking up in silence at a man suspended between earth and sky.

I do not know how long he hung there in the strange hot wind against that steel-grey sky, for after a while I turned and made my way slowly down the hillside.

'Were you there when they crucified my Lord?' Always now I should have to say that I was—and I did not know whether I would say it in shame or in exultation.

CHAPTER II

ARTS AND CRAFTS OF CENTRAL MEXICO

ONE MORNING the telephone rang; it was William Deneen.

'We're leaving on another trip today,' he said. 'I want to find a village called Santa Maria del Rio where they make silk *rebozos*—oh, and lots of other things—all in Central Mexico. What about coming with us? You can? Splendid! We'll pick you up about eleven o'clock then.'

William and Bill and the station wagon seemed like old friends this time as we drove out of Mexico City by the leafy avenue of Reforma, which was crowded with families on holiday because it was Mothers' Day. (In San Angel there had been a queue half a mile long stretching from the school where Mothers' Day parcels from the President were being distributed. Wrapped in flowered paper and labelled, 'To the Mothers of Mexico', each contained, among other things, flour, sugar, cloth and a blue zinc cooking pot. Sons and husbands stood on the fringes of the queue with their bicycles to carry the parcel home. This was going on all over Mexico.)

'I'd hate to run over a mother on Mothers' Day!' exclaimed Bill who was driving, as a *rebozoed* figure, with a child at each heel, stepped out into the road in front of us without a glance to right or left.

It was evening before we saw San Miguel Allende, a lovely cluster of steeples and domes, lying below us in a valley. It was a little gem of a town, full of old Colonial houses with heavily carved doors, and from every little alley came the tapping of craftsmen beating out gold or silver. For once the music that drifted out from the open doors was not all 'juke-box', but also snatches of guitar music that was truly Mexican.

We put up for the night at the Institute San Miguel Allende, a Cultural Summer School (but also an hotel), where the art rooms opened off lovely patios with plashing fountains.

In the Painting Room, half-finished canvases were grouped round a tableau consisting of a sagging sheet on a couple of poles, a few leaves, a piece of red paper and a stool. My imagination instantly converted this into an entire Mexican market; so apparently did everyone else's for I noticed then that half the canvases depicted exactly that.

On the notice board outside were various interesting items from, 'Kittens ready to leave their mother', to 'Trip on horseback to Laredo for someone with very little luggage'.

The little *zocalo* of San Miguel, with its round clipped trees and fretted silver-painted seats, was dominated by a church intended to be Gothic; as only the top half had been on the drawing only the top half had been built, so it was all spires and no body.

Once we left San Miguel the plains that encompassed us were so vast that we could see eight oxen teams ploughing at once. Each was composed of two yoked oxen. Behind them they dragged a primitive one-handled, one-furrowed wooden plough such as the Mexican Indians have used for centuries. The ploughman kept one hand on the plough and in the other balanced a long goad with a sharp iron tip with which he occasionally prodded the flank of the oxen; behind walked a 'clod-hopper', breaking up the clods with a long wooden hammer.

Groups of cattle moved slowly along the roadside in a small cloud of dust, foraging what they could from the dry edges. Little tornadoes were continually spiralling across the plain; once I counted fourteen in succession.

'Not surprising,' remarked William. 'I saw in the paper yesterday that they've been sending out tornado warnings for Texas and Oklahoma!'

As we left the plains behind, bare mountain peaks rose all round us; between them lay river valleys darkly green with maize.

Somewhere in these mountains was the village we were looking for—Santa Maria del Rio. We stopped to ask the way of an old Indian, whose donkey had a wooden plough slanted across his back as if he was carrying his cross.

Santa Maria? The old man indicated a track on the right. It wound between high mountain walls for several miles but, finally, like a well-kept secret, revealed a tiny closely-knit village. In the rather unkempt *zocalo* overhung by tall trees we found the *Rebozo* School.

The Director was out on his bicycle, but a boy who could identify it was sent with us and we set off in search of it. He directed us up tiny earth roads between high peeling plaster walls where our bumpers sometimes scraped on both sides. Every now and then the boy thought he saw the Director's bicycle outside one of the *adobe* houses, or disappearing down the end of a narrow street, but closer examination when we had chased after it always proved him wrong. At last, however, he gave a shout of triumph and pointed to one leaning up against a wooden door. Sure enough when he rapped loudly a thin-faced man with a dark moustache appeared at the window. The situation was explained, and, after a short consultation with someone inside, the Director emerged, shook hands with us and climbed into the back of the car, while the boy mounted the bicycle and rode ahead.

The Director told us he had about twenty weavers and would be delighted to show us the whole process of making the fine silk *rebozos* for which Santa Maria del Rio is famous.

In the courtyard with its ferns, three or four young women were seated winding the silk on to reels. (Nowadays many *rebozos* are made of artificial silk but the pure silk ones, which are much rarer and very expensive, are so fine that they can be threaded through a wedding ring.)

In a yard at the back a woman was preparing a deep luminously red dye, dipping the silk yarn into it and hanging it up to dry in long lines. The Indians have always made wonderful natural dyes from plants, especially from the cochineal insect which lives on the *nopal* cactus.

In an upper room four girls with long black plaits were seated on rush-covered chairs in front of their looms singing a part-song as they worked; as with all Mexican music a melancholy undercurrent ran through it, and the lovely harmonizing drifted out into a patio which framed a distant view of mountains and trees. Two of the girls had their looms out here. One, about eighteen, her glossy plaits falling down her pale mauve dress, her dark liquid eyes intent on her shuttle, was weaving a *rebozo* of pale green and fawn; the other was plaiting the silk fringes of a violet one. Hanging over the loom were two which they had just finished—one of palest rose, the other of aquamarine, both as soft to the touch as a spider's web. Great pottery jars of flowering plants had already turned the patio into a stage set long before William and Bill transformed it into one with the movie cameras.

Meantime the Director had sent a boy out to fetch *refrescoes* for us and he arrived back hugging half-a-dozen bottles of Coca-Cola. The caps were knocked off and we sat on the shady side of the patio drinking from our respective bottles, watched with interest by all the other weavers who had left their looms and were peering out from every doorway to see what was going on.

That night as we sat having supper in San Luis Potosí, the man at the next table turned out to be the manager of a zinc mine.

'Why not come over to the smelting yard in the morning,' he suggested. 'I'd be pleased to show you round.'

We drove over after breakfast and found trucks unloading piles of jagged red stone; Indians, in trousers and straw hats, their brown skin glistening with perspiration, were breaking up the stone with sledge hammers and shovelling it into a crusher where the fine grain was extracted. 'If you like I'll send one of the men with you to the mines,' suggested the manager. 'It's not far.'

He detailed one of the workmen to jump in the back of the car, which the man did most willingly, glad to be out of the burning sun for a while. It was a rough flinty track into the mountains and after twenty or thirty miles William began to get a bit restive. 'How much further?' he kept asking: the answer was always the same, '*Muy cerca!*' (very near). There was always a dizzy drop on our near-side as great valleys fell away one after the other. The only thing we saw was a mule, its two front legs hobbled, hopping across the road as if taking part in a two-legged race.

Finally, however, we came to a few huts. The Indian, his face beaming, announced that we were there. He told us that it was considered unlucky for women to go down the mine here, so I had to wait above ground while William and Bill, wearing steel helmets, clambered into a rickety cage and dropped out of sight.

Apart from the mine huts the only sign of life was a little stone hut with an old palm thatch. This was the café and the couple of Indians sitting on the one wooden bench eating *tacos* were almost eclipsed under the largest hats I had yet seen, tied on at the back with a black string with a dangling black tassel. They moved up on the bench to make room for me, staring at me with frank curiosity and we were just beginning a conversation over my bottle of *Sidral Mundet* (apple juice) when a shout from outside made us look round. A fine old man with a heavy curled moustache had just ridden up on a black mule; his feet were encased in engraved leggings that were part of the silver studded saddle from which hung a lassoo. His name was Primitivo Carenas, he was seventy-three years old, and he had just made a three-hour journey across the mountains from his little *rancho* to have a drink at the café, his nearest habitation.

Afterwards I wandered out on to the mountainside and sat in the shade of a gigantic *nopal* cactus whose leaves, edged with blossom, were backlit by the sun into blazing circles of orange and red. All round me, enfolded in a deep silence, lay the crags and peaks of the Sierra Madre.

Meantime, the man in charge of pulling up the cage in the mine was having a siesta. Twenty feet up in mid-air he was stretched out full length on a narrow length of board jutting out into space; had he moved an inch either way he must have fallen off it. However, he was lying on his side sleeping peacefully. Finally a whistle sounded and the cage was hauled up. It had been muddy, dark and damp down there. 'No supports whatever in that perfect labyrinth of galleries!' exclaimed William. However there had been a shrine, complete with artificial flowers, to which all the miners had doffed their helmets as they passed.

Back in San Luis Potosí we set out towards Aguascalientes across more vast plains. Mountains were now nothing but a delicate pencil sketch on the horizon; the sun-scorched earth gave out a steady radiance, and the *nopal* cacti were almost luminous. Suddenly a cloud crossed the sun; instantly the scene was colourless, then, as swiftly, swept back into brilliance again. Though there was nothing but earth and cactus, yet that transition from sun to shadow and back again was as dramatic as if it had been over a bed of tulips.

In Aguascalientes the hotel, though inexpensive, had a black marble staircase wide enough to grace a palace, but my main recollection of the town is of an old Indian woman walking across the *zocalo* with her empty bread basket upside down on her head for shade, and looking as dignified as a queen.

'What I want to find now is that little village of Tonalá where they make the pottery, and Paracho where they make the guitars,' said William over breakfast. 'Let's see how far it is on the map, Bill.'

'We could fit both those in if we took this route from Guadalajara,' said Bill, studying the map. 'Then we could drive alongside Lake Chapala too. I heard someone say the water hyacinths have nearly blocked it up so we'd better see it while we can!'

In Guadalajara fine wide streets like Avendida Juárez were lined with shops and it was all very modern, but the squares with their fountains and trees and massive stone churches gave an old-world touch to it, so did the few hansom cabs clip-clopping about.

Not far away we found the tiny village of Tonalá. Almost every backyard was a potter's workshop and the small untidy plaza was a checkerboard of pottery laid out on the ground. The inhabitants of Tonalá must spend their lives making pottery and then selling it to each other.

In one of the earth yards we watched a potter hard at work in the shade of a *mesquite* tree. He was shaping a clay jug by means of a footwheel. When finished it had to stand for three hours in the sun before it could be painted and glazed and was then baked in an old kiln which stood in the corner of the yard and was kept burning with cow dung and charcoal. When painting he just took his brush and painted anything that came into his head. Some of his finished work was incredibly beautiful—enormous glazed brown plates with patterns of black feathers, birds, or flowers.

On our way through the next village of Tlaquepaque we sat in the little *zocalo* on basket chairs of criss-crossed blackened pigskin and drank a *refresco*, before driving on to Lake Chapala. At once seven or eight *mariachis* (musicians) gathered round us, all elderly men in old white cotton suits and huge hats; six had fiddles or guitars, one had a 'cello. For a *peso* a man per song they volunteered to give us a private entertainment. The big fat one did most of the verse singing; one with a mournful countenance did nothing but run two fingers back and forth across the strings of his guitar, having carefully hung his half-smoked cigar on a hook on the end of it. However the combined result, once they all got into their stride, was amazingly tuneful, though hardly 'private', for as soon as they struck the first chord a small crowd appeared from nowhere, and soon pressed round so closely that, sitting down in the midst of it, we began to get claustrophobia.

Next day we reached Lake Chapala. It was so vast that I thought for a moment that we had taken a wrong turning and come out at the Gulf.

'Well, I must say there doesn't look much wrong with it at the moment!' remarked Bill.

However, as we drove on isolated patches of water hyacinths began to appear, gradually increasing till they were like a green plain stretching out into the lake, sometimes covered so closely with blossom that it resembled a vast lawn of mauve daisies. Not only are the hyacinths beginning to block up the lake; they are also killing the white fish for which Chapala is famous.

As we climbed up into the mountains we came to cactus country again—this time acres of the blue *tequila* cactus, finer-leafed than the more powerful looking *pulque*-producing *maguey*.

From the *tequila* cactus are distilled the two famous Mexican drinks—both very potent—*tequila* and *mescal*.

In Zamora where we stayed that night there was a fiesta in progress and the narrow streets were hung like a curtain with strips of cut paper. The little tree-shaded *zocalo* was all excitement, light and movement, with a band playing in the centre and promenading in progress. Two rows of girls were walking one way, two rows of young men the other, while flower sellers had stationed themselves in between the two at intervals. Now and then a young man would leave his companions and dart across to buy a single rose or carnation. He would then walk on till he came face to face with a girl he fancied, and hand the flower to her as they passed; if she was wearing it next time round they would exchange a smile and a bow; the time after they would begin to walk round together.

'Well, just look at that fellow, will you!' exclaimed Bill, as one young man bought a whole bunch of roses, put all except one behind his back, and then gallantly presented one to each of a dozen different girls; he then examined them more closely on the next round to make up his mind which one he really preferred.

In the centre children were promenading round the bandstand; tiny girls skipped round joyously in pairs with linked hands; fathers walked round awkwardly with small sons. Everybody was walking somewhere, even though it was only in a circle.

In the State of Michoacán next day we saw wheat being cut by hand, and mules being driven round and round in an enclosure to tread out the grain; donkeys carried the sheaves packed into wide-meshed nets like round gold pumpkins. By contrast we met a huge combine harvester lumbering along the road on its way to one of the larger farms.

Soon we were up among pine forests, and for the rest of the day the fragrance of the forests was always with us. It was here that we found Paracho, a little village lying tucked away in a valley, its wooden houses all overhung with heavy eaves. Women were pushing little handcarts especially made to hold two enormous pottery water jars, and donkeys had special wooden frames fitted to their saddles to hold these jars. All the older men had shaggy moustaches and wore nigger-brown *zarapes*, and their cone-shaped straw hats with huge brims were held on by a black cord.

There was the fragrance of sawn wood everywhere for every pavement in the little earth streets propped up rows of thin board ready for guitar-making, and almost every house was a family 'factory'. The equipment was simply a few tools, a charcoal iron and a bucket of water. We watched a boy cutting out guitar handles with a sharp knife and fitting them on to the frames; then with a heated iron bar he bent strips of wet wood to form the sides. Guitars in various stages of assembly leaned up against all the whitewashed walls. Some of the more expensive were finished off with rings of inlaid mother-of-pearl, and before we left William bought a particularly fine one.

Not far from the village was Mexico's youngest volcano, Paricutin, which appeared out of nowhere one day in 1943. A peasant of this State of Michoacán, walking across his field, suddenly became aware of a trembling under his feet like a cooking *tortilla*, and of small puffs of smoke. Without waiting to investigate he took to his heels, and so can now claim the distinction of being the only living individual to witness the birth-throes of a volcano, for seven hours later Paricutin was spewing out molten lava over the surrounding countryside. The motto is if you feel anything suspicious happening under your feet don't poke at it to see what it is—just run! Dr. Atl, true to his title of Mexico's Painter of Volcanoes, promptly bought the field in which Paricutin had so unexpectedly reared up, and settled down in a hut to paint its progress.

As we passed Lake Pátzcuaro later that day there was an illusion of many gigantic butterflies hovering above the surface because all the fishing boats were using twin nets, like great round wings, that dipped and rose constantly.

Near Toluca a few days later we visited a tiny basket-making village. At the first house we drew a blank. The weaver did not work on Tuesdays—and this was Tuesday.

'You see,' explained his wife, 'my husband drinks much *pulque* on Sunday, so he must rest on Monday and Tuesday to be able to work hard on Wednesday, Thursday, Friday and Saturday.'

Further on we were lucky. The weaver here indulged in his *pulque* on a Saturday, rested on Sunday and Monday, and was on top form by Tuesday.

Eight people were living in the tiny *adobe* house of two rooms; the only furniture was their *petate* mats, a wooden table, a couple of old kitchen chairs and a small altar with the rear light of a cycle fixed up over a framed picture of the Virgin of Guadalupe. In the smaller room there was a charcoal fire for cooking and a pile of maize cobs and beans. The little yard at the back was divided from the maize field by a hedge of *nopal* cactus, now a mass of orange, yellow and pink blossom.

The weaver, Ignacio, was helped by his two sons, the three of them forming a basket 'factory' in their back yard. He told us he had to go eight miles by donkey to fetch his reeds, and showed us how they had first to be soaked well in a tin bath, then spread out in the sun to dry before being split with a finger nail. Then, seated in the shade of the huge cactus, and overshadowed by its exotic blossoms, father and sons settled down to work, each grasping a handful of split palms. Meantime the flies bit us unmercifully for, in spite of its glamorous background of flowers, the yard was far from clean since there was no sanitation whatever. All the family had been born in that house, and Ignacio's father had been a weaver there before him. Later he showed us all sorts of baskets he had made ranging from tiny ones for coins to huge ones with lids for luggage; these he took into Toluca and sold in the market.

Many miles beyond Toluca was Taxco, the chief silver-making village. It lay like a mountain fortress surrounded by its silver mines. In ancient workrooms like catacombs we watched the silver being beaten out by hand with the rounded end of a hammer into the most elaborate necklaces and bracelets.

As we drove back along the winding mountain road, children, and sometimes adults, would suddenly pop out from behind a rock or a tree with an iguana—an enormous lizard—on the end of a piece of string. Some would dangle it hopefully in front of the approaching car like a fish on a rod; others would put it on their head to attract your attention; while some would throw it on the road in front of you and draw it away just as you reached it. The main thing of course was that you should feel induced to possess it, either as a pet or to eat.

When at last we drew up in San Angel again I felt as if I had been away for months.

'We'll be going up to Guanajuato later on to see the plays they put on in the streets there every year,' said William as we said goodbye. 'I'll let you know when it is. You may like to come with us.'

CHAPTER 12

TULA AND CHOLULA

SOMETIMES I would spend the day at Tula, the ancient capital of the Toltecs, about fifty miles north of Mexico City. The train passed through a strange network of canyons on the way, a fantasy land of stalactites and stalagmites, partly soil erosion, partly the remains of a gigantic trench over four miles long which had been cut through the hills by the Spaniards in an endeavour to lessen the floods which afflicted Mexico City every rainy season. It was never successful, and now you can hardly distinguish it from the natural ravines and erosion.

In the little streets of Tula village, bordered by ash trees, many houses had lovely fragments of sculpture from the ruins, embedded into their walls; for after the City of Tollan, or Tula, was destroyed by fire in A.D. 1150 it was continually being looted, beginning with the Aztecs who took a lot of its sculptures and incorporated them into Tenochtitlan, their own capital.

Just beyond the village lay a wide river and this was my favourite way up to the ruins. The only way to cross it was by a long thin suspension bridge, just a succession of small boards nailed together, many of them loose, some missing altogether; a thin strand of wire on either side served as a handhold. It was easy enough to negotiate if you were alone, and trod in such a way that you did not make it swing, but sometimes when I was half-way across a couple of women with brown water jars on their shoulders would advance on to it from the other end—or worse, a heavy-footed peasant with a sack of maize on his head. Then the bridge would sway sideways, up and down and back and forth all at the same time so that it was like trying to walk on a sliding deck, but with only two thin strands of wire between you and the green depths far below.

Once across it I would take one of the little stony tracks, nothing more than channels, that led up steeply through a maze of cacti. Some of the *nopal* here were so tall that the orange and yellow blossoms round the edge of their disc-like leaves, caught by the sun, looked from a distance like fairy lights on a Christmas tree. The few habitations here were nothing but piled-up stones, or a few boards draped with *maguey* leaves for a roof.

I would come out on a stony plateau dotted with more cacti, some like small rounded heads, others like great candelabra, and from there I would get my first glimpse of Tula, its four huge Atlantean figures on top of the Pyramid silhouetted against the sky. These enormous figures, about eighteen feet high and carved of grey stone, each represented a Warrior wearing a butterfly-type breast-plate. His head-band, covered in stars, ended in a bunch of carved feathers; his face had once been painted and the deep-set eye sockets, once inlaid and now empty, gave him the appearance of wearing glasses. He wore a bead necklace and a belt with a great clasp at the back engraved with the sun and four serpents; his only item of clothing was an embroidered breech-clout. In one hand he held a dart-thrower, in the other a cluster of darts, and he also carried a curved sword and a bag for holding incense. Each of these figures was carved in four sections which fitted together by means of a tenon and mortise. I think they seemed so extraordinarily realistic because their knees, though each about the size of a normal person's head, were beautifully curved and rounded, and their toe-nails were sharply defined.

For all their colossal size they had such a calm and beneficent air that I felt most at ease with them, and this was as it should be since they represent Quetzalcoatl, the good and wise Deity of Culture and Brotherhood in his role of Venus, the Morning Star. His opposite number in the pantheon of gods was Tezcatlipoca, the Smoking Mirror, God of Evil-doing and Night. As Mexico's famous archeologist, Alfonso Caso says, 'These two deities are at war, and their struggles are the history of the Universe.'

The Stone Warriors, representing the god Quetzalcoatl, on top of the Toltec Pyramid at Tula

The statue of Saint Francis in the garden of the *hacienda*, Guanajuato

He had ridden for three hours over the mountains for a drink and a chat
at the nearest café . . .

The café. State of San Luis Potosí

In the end Tezcatlipoca seems to have won as far as the Toltecs of Tula were concerned for they became so decadent that tradition tells that Quetzalcoatl could stand it no longer and in A.D. 987 he left them, though he prophesied that one day he would return. He reappeared in Yucatán where, in the Mayan ruins of Chichén Itzá, there are Toltec symbols representing Quetzalcoatl identical to many of these at Tula. I determined to go to Yucatán and see them for myself. (Eventually I did too—but that's another story.)

Apparently the Spaniards never saw these great Stone Warriors of Tula. During recent excavations here archeologists drove a tunnel right through the centre of the pyramid and discovered that at some time prior to the Conquest it had been deliberately opened and the interior emptied.

Inside, in sections, they found these Atlantean figures which had once held up the temple roof.

Now, sitting on top of the Pyramid of Quetzalcoatl, leaning against the feet of one of them, as they stand guard again over the valley of Tula, I could look right across to the notched hill called Xicuco, the Crooked Hill. It was because of that hill that the Toltecs had called this capital of theirs Tollan Xicocotitlan.

Eventually the Toltecs themselves had been overthrown by wild tribes from the north, among them the Aztecs who, though partly responsible for the burning of Tollan (or Tula) held the Toltecs in great respect as architects and took over much of their culture. After the fall of Tenochtitlan and the Aztec Empire in 1521 the Spaniards allowed Don Pedro Moctezuma, son of the Emperor Moctezuma, to live at Tula. Thanks to letters which he wrote in Latin much is known about Tula during the Aztec period.

A few other things besides the Warriors had survived fire and plunder. In a narrow slit of a passage behind the Pyramid I found a wall where some of the original facing had survived. The carved stone slabs were engraved with eagles devouring human hearts; human faces emerged from the fangs of a plumed serpent; and there was a whole procession of tigers. There were also several cement drains, in fact the drainage system all over Tula had been so excellent that during the recent excavations they only had to remove the accumulated silt of centuries, and the drains immediately began to function perfectly, and have been carrying off the water during the rainy season ever since.

Round the other side of the Pyramid was the Palace of Quetzalcoatl and there, where the *adobe* walls still bore traces of that tremendous fire of A.D. 1150, something else had survived—part of an exquisitely painted bench that had once run the length of the wall. It showed a procession of thirteen Toltec chiefs in magnificent head-dresses, wearing skirts and carrying shields. Their flesh was tinted a pale orange, ornaments were red, feathers blue and yellow. After centuries, not to mention the heat of the fire, these original colours were still vivid and beautiful—in fact this bench is one of the most precious remains of Toltec art in Mexico.

Far below me in the valley I could see the smoke from a factory, where the same ingredients which the Toltecs used to pave these courtyards and plaster these walls are now being used to make Tolteca cement. Apart from this, where once a whole Empire had held sway now there was nothing but stony hills dotted with cactus, and a silence that was unbroken save for the occasional whistle of a barefooted Indian boy driving his goats between the ruins of a pyramid and a palace.

Now that I had found Tula I was anxious to see Cholula, south of Mexico City. Quetzalcoatl, between his disappearance from Tula and his reappearance in Yucatán, is said to have stopped there for twenty years to give his teachings to the Cholulans, who became a cultured and artistic people and erected in his honour what is said to be the largest pyramid in the world.

One day I took a bus to Puebla, intending to spend a night or two there and find my way to Cholula. I was just leaving the small hotel in the morning when a young man came up to me.

'Good morning,' he said. 'May I speak some words with you? My name is Jaime and I am friend for the son of this hotel. I am so interested to speak some English words because I am studying it in my home.'

Exploring Puebla

When Jaime discovered that I did not yet know Puebla he insisted on showing me the lay-out of the town. 'I am Boy Scout,' he said. 'I like very much to helping people.'

He seemed to know everyone in Puebla, and all the way down the street we were greeted by one friend after another who shook hands with me with a '*Mucho gusto, señorita*' (Much pleasure), to which I replied likewise, '*Mucho gusto.*' Even if no more was said we then all shook hands again before parting.

'At one o'clock I shall take you to see our *fronton* Club,' said Jaime. 'Every day with three friends I am playing there. It is a sport much played in Mexico. Afterwards I shall explain you how to go to Cholula. *Adios, señorita. Mucho gusto!*'

I spent the morning exploring Puebla with ease now that I had my bearings. In the factory that made the famous Talavera tiles, with which the façades of many of the lovely old Colonial houses of Puebla and Mexico City are covered, I watched small boys treading the clay with bare feet, while an old artist sat cross-legged painting the tiles by hand.

In the streets here there were many of the windowless shops opening directly on to the pavement; at night, metal shutters come down as a protection, though they can sometimes be more of a menace since, once safely inside, thieves can work undetected behind them.

Once I came upon a display of tier upon tier of coffins. These are very elaborate in Mexico, being covered in pleated and quilted grey silk inside and out, and finished off with big tassels; tiny ones for children are done in the same way but in white silk.

At one o'clock I met Jaime in the *zocalo* and we went out to the *fronton* (hardball) court with its tremendously high wall on three sides. It was a strenuous game in which the ball was flung with speed and force from an oval basket-like container strapped to the wrist and caught in it again with a terrific impact.

Afterwards he showed me where to catch a bus for Cholula. 'I shall call at eight o'clock tonight and see if you have found yourself well there,' he said gravely, shaking hands with me.

Cholula is actually one of the most historical places in Mexico, yet if you passed through it in a bus you might not give it a second glance. The streets with their broken pavements, flat-roofed houses and almost windowless plaster walls are blank-faced, and, on this particular day at any rate, were so filled with flying dust that all the women I met were holding the edges of their *rebozos* across their mouths, and no babies' heads were permitted to emerge from their wrappings.

What looked at first like an enormous natural hill dominating the town, crowned by a large white church, turned out to be the *Tepanapa*, the largest pyramid in the world. Consisting of seven pyramids, each completely enclosing the last as a different culture predominated, it was covered up by the Spaniards to hide it, and also so that they could surmount it with a Christian church.

It was a long hot climb up the dusty hillside, but once there I had a most magnificent view. On the skyline stood Popocatépetl and Ixtaccíhuatl, and every inch of the ground between seemed to be cultivated in little strips, mostly *maguey*, while immediately below me lay Cholula, spread out like a fan. But what a difference now! Instead of dust and blankness there was an almost dizzying impression of domes in every size and colour. Some people claim that Cholula has three hundred and sixty-five churches. I did not manage to count as many as that though I got up to fifty. They even appeared as lonely outposts in the fields around, for when the Spaniards arrived in 1519 Cholula was known to the Indians as the Holy City of Anáhuac (the Indian name for the Valley of Mexico), and was one of the most flourishing ceremonial centres on the Plateau and a Mecca for pilgrimages. It then had a population of some fifty thousand, but this was quickly decimated by the Spaniards in a terrible massacre of reprisal because the Cholulans had planned to ambush them on their way to Tenochtitlan. The Spaniards then tore down all the pyramids and temples of Cholula —or, in the case of the biggest one simply covered it up with earth —and built a church on the site of each. The one that fascinated me was the Franciscan Church of San Gabriel which, from the hilltop, looked like a Moorish mosque with its forty-seven domes all connected to form one enormous vaulted roof.

Deep down inside the 'hill' on which I was standing several miles of tunnels have now been bored penetrating right into the seven pyramids within it. I scrambled down the hillside by a winding track on the other side and found a small dark opening which was the entrance to these tunnels. The dark-eyed Cholulan in charge who was squatting on the ground outside pocketed my *peso*, picked up a torch, and pulled down a couple of switches at the entrance. Immediately a thin trail of lights flashed up revealing a narrow tunnel that melted away into distance.

'*Con permiso, señorita,*' he said, and led the way into it.

Other tunnels soon began to branch out from the original one and as we turned one corner after another I soon lost track of which way we had come; the tunnel was so narrow in places that I could touch roof and both walls at the same time. Now and again we would come to complete darkness ahead; then, with '*Un momentito, señorita*', my guide would disappear with his torch into the blackness. After a few moments I would hear a click, then another thin trail of light would come on ahead.

At times he would stop to point out sections of the different pyramids—Toltec, Olmec, etc.—for the tunnels, artificially constructed of *adobe* and stone, are so arranged that you traverse different levels and see parts of each pyramid in turn. One moment we would be looking at part of Pyramid No. 6, next moment we were climbing up five or six roughly-made steps for a look at No. 4. We would carry on for a few tunnels to a section of No. 3, then dip down to No. 2. One section would be Toltec, another Olmec, and so on, but I had a hard job to sort out which was which for if I stopped too long making notes, I was liable to look up and find that my guide had gone on and I was alone in the tunnel. Since he meticulously turned off the lights behind him I was not anxious to get left too far behind.

One thing I remember was the thrill of turning a corner and coming upon a series of painted wall frescoes. Some of the figures had strange skull-like faces resembling grasshoppers, but the colours were as vivid as though they had been painted yesterday. Since they were on the wall of Pyramid No. 1 the innermost of the seven, they had been there for well on two thousand years.

Because the Indians always used natural colours,—crushing up plants, minerals or insects and mixing the powder with oil or water—their colours never faded. All the figures in these ancient Indian murals are the same size whether close at hand or distant, because the artists did not know or trouble much about perspective; they were much more concerned with portraying strength and grace through their brush-strokes and in achieving an overall pleasing and colourful effect. Their painting did not appeal much to the Spaniards who were used to the more realistic European art—and in any case they were more concerned with getting the Indians to build churches and work in the fields and mines. So after the Conquest this ancient art slowly died out.

When finally we wound our way back through the labyrinth, I emerged blinking in the strong sunlight. As I walked slowly down the dusty road towards the town I stopped to look back. There was nothing to see except a parched hill with a few pepper trees. Ridiculous to think that ten minutes ago I had been standing *inside* it looking at wall frescoes!

I spent the rest of the day going from one church to another till my neck ached with looking up into domes and my eyes were dizzy with gazing at façades that ranged from the most elaborate baroque style to the simplicity of some derelict chapel.

Originally the Spaniards had provided only small open chapels for the Indians since they were used to worshipping in the open at the foot of their pyramids, but their own churches, built with forced Indian labour—and often, as with the Cathedral of Mexico City, with the very stones from the pyramid they had forced the Indians to pull down—were very elaborate. At first they were more like fortresses in case of uprisings by the Indians, but later as the Indians grew more subdued and friendly, the Spaniards began to give these churches beautiful *plateresque* façades (so called because the carving round the big doors was as delicate as the work of the silversmiths). Later came the fantastic baroque and the even more elaborate *churrigueresca* style, the latter an almost solid mass of decoration. Two of Mexico's most beautiful baroque churches, Santa Maria Tonanzintla and San Francisco Ecatepec, lie just outside Cholula.

Inevitably, after Mexican Independence from Spain, there was a swing in the opposite direction; buildings became neo-classic, more after the Greek and Roman style but, as a whole, Mexican people still prefer the baroque.

When I had had my fill of churches—long before the supply was exhausted I am afraid—I wandered out into the *maguey* plantations, following the dusty tracks with their scatterings of grey box-like *adobe* houses. Sometimes where the heart of a great plant had been hacked out I would lift the piece of broken stone that covered it and find myself looking down into an ivory bowl of clear *agua miel* which had not yet had it's day's 'milking'. Almost every one of these tracks, however small or dusty, had a derelict church at one end or the other, in fact Cholula can be conjured up for me now by four words—churches, dust, *maguey* and tunnels.

I got back to Puebla in a rackety little second-class bus and found my way back to the hotel.

There was no sign of Jaime by half-past eight, nor by nine, but I simply put this down to the vagaries of Mexican time. Not at all! When he finally arrived, he was breathless and dishevelled, his arm was bandaged from elbow to wrist, and it transpired that he had been knocked down by a car after leaving the office and had had to be bandaged up at the hospital. Instead of going straight home he had taken the trouble to come right down to the hotel to see if I had got on all right at Cholula, and also to tell me that he had met an old school friend who was now a doctor at the hospital.

'I was telling him that you were from England,' added Jaime, 'and he said that if you like to come with me in the morning when I must go back for another injection he would be very happy to show you all the hospital. It is one of our new Social Security ones,' he finished proudly.

Next morning Jaime's doctor friend, who was not due to perform his next operation till midday, took me to see the operating theatres which all had large windows facing the mountains and also had music laid on.

'When we operate we can turn our eyes sometimes and see the hills,' he explained, 'also we can have what music we wish. I always have Bach when I am operating.'

In the children's ward lunch was being prepared—soup, beef, potatoes and melon—on individual aluminium trays with scooped-out sections. The children looked so happy that I commented on it. The doctor smiled.

'That is our trouble,' he said; 'they don't want to go home again! Often the mother of a poor family will keep her child without water all day so that it will get fever and have to come into hospital. She knows it will get good food and become well and fat. Sometimes they even bring them in and don't collect them again! I like so much working with these little Indian children,' he added. 'You see what eyes they have? Like black cherries! When you have to give them some treatment you will see the eyes of the little Indian boy turn to his father as if to say, "May I complain? May I cry?"; the father's eyes will say sternly, "No!" Then there is no fuss, no tears. It is the ones who are getting into civilization who complain! But we have to remember always with the Indians that they have that background of the conqueror —the heart of the Indian was broken long ago. We complain about their stealing, but they never know if the hate is coming again. With the pure Indians of the north it is different. Those few tribes who remain were never conquered. They walk on their own level and look at us from that level.'

In the adult wards most of the men who could sit up were reading comics, or the cheap paper-back picture novels so popular in Mexico.

'But we have now started a trolley with books to try and get them to read something better,' said the doctor. 'You notice we have to keep this outside door locked—that is so that no *pulque* can be smuggled in! If they are thirsty they can have *Sidral Mundet* or tea with lemon—but no coffee.'

Downstairs he showed me the blood bank.

'Everybody coming in for an operation has to bring someone with him to give an equal amount of blood,' he explained. 'It may not be the same type of blood as the patient's but it is to replace what we use from here. Sometimes I get a patient who says, "Doctor, they say I must have an operation and I've nobody to bring for the blood." Then I have to go to the Director and say that in this case it must be done without. If the blood bank runs short we ask the Unions to give extra donations. It is easier for the hospitals in Mexico City. Many people donate there because they get paid for it; for instance, students who need extra *pesos* for a party will go along and give some blood.'

'How are the expenses covered here?' I asked.

'The Government gives a third for each patient,' he replied, 'the employer a third and the patient a third. This is what we call a Social Security Zone Hospital. We have smaller clinics around, but patients can come here for X-rays.'

As we left, patients were passing in and out of the entrance hall to the accompaniment of the clicking of a slot machine selling refrigerated Coca-Cola.

By complete contrast to the dust and churches of Cholula the following week found me in Acapulco—Mexico's favourite tropical Pacific coast resort. I woke up several times on my first night there to hear soft thuds outside. Next morning before breakfast I picked up twenty-four ripe yellow mangoes, still with the bloom on them, from the lawn outside my window. That garden at Acapulco, which belonged to a friend I had got to know in Mexico City, reminded me of the Tropical House at Kew. There were breadfruit trees, pomegranates, vanilla vines, cocoanuts, and cachou nuts that looked like broad beans sticking up on top of a small oval orange fruit. Loofas hung down from their vine like marrows; when you peeled off the skin, there was just fibre inside. Once it was dry you could cut it up and use it at the kitchen sink.

The beaches of Acapulco were equally exotic, their golden sands dotted with small tables each with a palm thatch. The water was like warm blue satin; there were water ski-ing contests and

Underwater Ballets; and one hotel even provided its guests with pink striped jeeps to drive themselves about in.

Sometimes when I returned from such a trip Mexico City would have undergone a botanical transformation. I remember the time I came back during March to find the misty mauve-blue jacaranda in blossom, and whole avenues canopied with what looked like inverted fields of bluebells.

One thing I looked forward to after all my journeys was the coming home to San Angel, for I always had such a welcome from Margarita and Mina, not to mention the parrot who knew me well by now.

I would settle down again for a while to what I thought of as Mexico City life—shopping in the market for papaya and limes; writing on my verandah in the sun; swimming in the pool; sunsets on the Pedregal; or just wandering round the city, which I never tired of doing.

Especially I looked forward to the evenings in the library with Margarita. Sometimes, sitting there with the lamplight glowing on the lovely bindings, I would get her to tell me about the many writers and artists who had visited her. There was the time, for instance, when Geraldine Farrar, the famous singer, came from New York to give a recital at Bellas Artes.

'She was one of the most beautiful women in the world,' remarked Margarita reflectively. 'She came here to lunch, and afterwards she offered to sing for us in here. She walked up those stairs and began to sing from the gallery. She had such a strong voice that the crystal chandelier began to quiver violently. It shook so much that she had to stop—we were afraid it would fall in pieces on us!'

She would talk to me of the Mexican writers and poets, many of whom she knew personally (her own brother, Edouard, was a poet), but there was one friend of hers in the literary world of whom she spoke more frequently than of any other, and that was Elena Cusi.

'She was so often in this library,' said Margarita. 'She would bring her poems and read them aloud for me. She wrote wonderful poetry . . . deep and powerful with thoughts, yet so tender . . . and always seeking. She was only forty-two when she died.'

She would take down a volume of Elena's poems and read them aloud for me, first in the original Spanish for the music of the words, then translating them into English. It was strong metaphysical poetry, magnificent in word and style, touching the mystery of death constantly . . . always asking . . . desperate for understanding. Her last work, a long poem entitled 'Psyche', was my favourite. It was sublimely beautiful. One knew that she had at last found the answers to all her questionings.

Many Mexican writers and artists lived in San Angel, and one day I was invited to tea by the painter, Carlos Tejeda, and his wife, Mercedes. I spent an absorbing afternoon in his studio looking at his fine portraits and vivid abstract paintings.

'Which is your favourite of all the portraits you have done?' I asked him at last.

For answer he went to a desk, took out a large photograph of an oil painting, and handed it to me.

It was a painting of sea and sky. Half merged within the clouds between them was the head of a beautiful young woman; her eyes were fixed steadfastly upon some unseen goal, and she seemed to be rising up from the horizon out of a dark sea just rippled with small white breakers. I find it impossible to convey my feelings as I looked at that portrait. I can only say that it made my heart beat faster, as certain notes of music do . . . that I just wanted to go on looking at it. But turn the pages and you will find it and you can test your own reactions.

'She was a dear friend of ours,' said Carlos Tejeda. 'When she came one day to have her portrait painted, I felt—I did not know why—that I must paint her like that, between water and sky. One month later she had a stroke. In eight months she was dead. She was a wonderful poet. Her name was Elena Cusi.'

CHAPTER 13

GUANAJUATO AND THE PLAYS

WILLIAM AND BILL called to collect me that week on their way to Guanajuato. It was evening when we arrived in the tiny medieval town which lies in a deep bowl of the mountains. We found rooms at the Posada Santa Fé overlooking the small *zocalo* with its circle of clipped laurels placed close together like upturned muffs. Unfortunately by the time we found our way to the Plaza de San Roque, that evening's Play was almost at an end. What we did see of it remained with me vividly.

The lamplit square, approached by narrow alleys, and with an old church as its background, formed a natural stage, and on the ground in attitudes of sleep or death—I did not know which—lay dozens of still figures in sixteenth-century costume. The audience, packed on raised wooden stands at one end of the square, was as still as the players.

Suddenly the square was plunged into darkness and a single spotlight focused upon a cobbled alley. A tall figure in black stood there. His cloak was lined with red silk, and as he slowly advanced into the square a drift of wind caught at it and swirled it into colour. As he threaded his way between the still figures on the ground the spotlight picked out lace at his throat and high cheekbones below the tall black hat.

He made his way towards the far side of the square while out of the darkness—seemingly from out of the sky—there came a deep resonant voice speaking an Epilogue in Spanish . . .

'. . . As his shadow is lost in the shadow of the street, his life

[160]

gone from the history of men, Cervantes is born into the second and the true life . . .'

At these words there came the soft tread of a horse on the cobbles and the spotlight picked out a Spanish knight riding slowly into the square; beside him on a donkey rode a smaller squat figure—it was Don Quixote and Sancho Panza. The two made their way between the prone figures and followed Cervantes into the darkness. For a few seconds, even when the sound of the hooves had died into distance, there was no sound from the audience. Then they began to applaud loudly.

Back in the hotel afterwards we met Licenciado Enrique Ruelas Espinosa, the producer, and his pretty dark-haired wife. He was short, with a little moustache, his dark hair receded from a high intelligent domed forehead and his brown eyes under the bushy eyebrows were keen and humorous. Though retired from his profession of lawyer he still teaches acting for the National Association of Actors.

'But how did you come to put on these plays in Guanajuato?' asked William.

Licenciado Ruelas smiled. 'Well, I took my title of lawyer here, and I felt very much about Guanajuato and its atmosphere of the sixteenth century. Always as I walked about the streets I could see cavaliers and ladies in silk! I needed to express what my imagination saw, so I started to write . . . to dream. I pictured an open-air theatre—but realistic, in the traditional life of the people. "Well, why don't I do it and use the streets and the houses?" I asked myself one day. So when I was made Director of the School of Dramatic Art here I selected first the *Entremesses* (sketches) of Cervantes to play—*he* used to walk about and dream too! That was eight years ago. Now we must continue every year for all the people want it. We use different streets for different plays, but the Plaza de San Roque where we were tonight is always used for Cervantes.'

'Any special reason?' I asked.

Licenciado Ruelas looked across at his wife; his brown eyes twinkled.

'Well yes! You see when I was studying here for a lawyer I loved someone from Guanajuato—she is now my wife! I had always to cross that plaza to visit her so it became rather special for me. That was why I chose it for Cervantes! It has not always been easy for the inhabitants in these Squares. They have to put up with a lot. They must not put on their lights or their radios when we are acting, and the actors must enter and depart from their houses. But, oh how good they have been with us! Once a man told us, "I'm sorry I cannot lend you my balcony this night because my wife is ill." When the evening came the actors forgot and went in. "Oh it is all right," he said; "my wife will cover her head while you go through the room to the balcony." '

'Of course,' he went on, 'although my actors are well trained I cannot always know what the animals will do! Once an actor's name was called, but before he could answer one of the donkeys gave a loud bray. "Heavens how his voice has changed!" exclaimed the first actor quickly. My biggest trouble is when some of my actors arrive a little drunk and have to be sobered up before they can go on. Then the play has to start late! Once I remember one of the soldiers had to carry a girl off the stage, but because he was a little drunk he carried off the wrong girl and she began screaming!'

'What about the time when the lights failed, Enrique!' put in his wife.

'Oh yes! Everything failed, even the spotlights! Then all the audience laughed and began to chant "Ruelas Ruelas, what happened with the *velas* (candles)?" I sent quickly for flaming torches, and the actors sang and the people sang with them—still no lights; so the actors made speeches, and some of the people got up and made speeches. It was a show in the middle of a show. Suddenly the electricity came back—and the play was running again. Once we were invited to make the *Entremesses* in Morelia, and quite an uneducated person came up to me and said indignantly, "Is it true you are going to take the *Entremesses* out of Guanajuato, Licenciado Ruelas? You cannot do that—they belong to Guanajuato!" Another time some children from the streets put on the plays themselves. They had watched us so often they had learnt it by heart!'

When I went up to bed William, Bill and Licenciado Ruelas were still talking plays and production.

'I've got a surprise for you,' said William when I came down to breakfast. 'Licenciado Ruelas and I had a long talk last night. He puts on his plays to help the town by attracting visitors—and I've always wanted a documentary film of a town like Guanajuato in the sixteenth century. So we're going to write up a script, using my cameras, and his actors, and the town as the setting! We'll shoot the scenes in the daytime as the actors will be busy every night. We're going to meet him after breakfast and work out all the details.'

We found Licenciado Ruelas waiting for us in the little café across the *zocalo*.

'This has been my "Office" for years,' he said, laughing, pulling up chairs for us; 'the proprietor says one day he will put a plaque on the wall! I have been thinking what we must do. You want to show Guanajuato as it was in the sixteenth century, also as it is now. The last is easy, but in the sixteenth century Guanajuato had some of the richest silver mines in Mexico—they kept the Spanish Treasury full for years! All round here were big *haciendas* (estates) of the Spaniards who owned them. That is one thing you *must* show—the inside of an *hacienda*.'

'But would we be able to?' asked William.

Licenciado Ruelas nodded. 'I know the owners of one of the biggest. I will have a word with them. Then, of course, you must show the silver mines as they were then with the Indians working in them, and the life of one of those Indians. For that we can go out to some village. Luckily it is vacation time for the University, so many of my actors are free in the daytime. We will all be pleased to help you—and Guanajuato will have some good publicity! First I will ring up the *hacienda*.'

He was back within five minutes. 'Fine, fine!' he exclaimed. 'We may go right away to see it.'

We drove out of Guanajuato and soon he directed William up a track into a desolate valley. There were no signs of even an *adobe* hut, let alone a 'great *hacienda*', though once we did see some ruins half hidden in the undergrowth and, further on, a high stone wall.

'Here we are!' exclaimed Licenciado Ruelas. He led the way to a heavy wooden door in the wall and pulled a bell. We heard footsteps, the door creaked open, and we stepped straight into another world. Avenues of cyprus, edged with grass like green velvet, stretched into a distance interwoven with rose gardens and fountains. Flights of rose-pink steps ascended between great urns of flowering cactus to a series of white arches cascading with bougainvillea like a shower of rubies, and framing a white sculptured Saint Francis of Assisi.

When half an hour later the huge wooden doors had closed behind us again and we stood on the dusty track with nothing visible but the high stone wall and the desolate valley, William, Bill and I looked at each other unbelievingly as if to say, 'Did *you* think you saw what *I* thought I saw?'

'Now you can imagine what wealth there was in the mines of Guanajuato that the Spaniards could build such places,' said Licenciado Ruelas.

We spent all afternoon in the café, building up a script . . . Our *hacendado* (owner) could have an official visit from the Spanish Viceroy—that would give us an excuse for a ball on the patio with minstrels.'And of course, being Mexicans, nearly all my actors can play the guitar,' put in Licenciado Ruelas, 'so *that* is no difficulty!'

After supper we went round to the Posada San Antonio for the Play of the Evening. Once a sixteenth-century inn, it is now a tenement dwelling for many families. The stands stood across one corner of the tiny courtyard and we climbed up to a fine, if precarious, seat on the top. There was no back, only a steep drop behind. Apart from a small rectangle of star-studded sky overhead, the high walls of the courtyard enclosed us like a well. The stands were quickly filled and late-comers had to put their cushions on the cobbles and sit there cross-legged. Soon the audience was bulging out on to the stage which was the cobbled floor of the courtyard plus the empty stables. Meantime families passing with

The oil portrait of Elena Cusi, Baroness de Imhoff, painted by
the Mexican artist, Carlos Tejeda

Ploughing a *milpa* (maize field) with oxen, Oaxaca

A *peso*, a man, a song: William and Bill listening to the *mariachis* in
Tlaquepaque

jugs or buckets along the balconies peered down at us through their lines of washing.

The play was scheduled to start at eight o'clock. At half-past eight the audience began to clap, not impatiently but just as a reminder that they were there. A donkey, secured to a ring in the wall, edged uncertainly back and forth and everyone sitting on the ground within range of his heels had to shift back and forth with him; a chicken tied to a stake in the cobbles by one leg, was equally restive.

At a quarter to nine the audience began to clap again. When this produced no results, two or three started a part song; soon the entire courtyard had taken it up—but there was still no sign of the actors. The donkey now lifted up his head and brayed loudly. As if that had been the signal all the lanterns went out. A spotlight shining on the donkey went out, then shone by mistake on some washing hanging on one of the balconies overhead, whereupon one of the unseen spectators, startled, dropped her bucket, fortunately empty, which rolled round the balcony with a clatter.

The play now began in earnest, each stable in turn being lit up and used as a setting. During a court scene—the court being the old hay barn fitted up with a refectory table and high backed chairs—the Judge had to interrogate prisoners while the Clerk took down their replies. In the middle there came another loud bray from the donkey. 'Now mind you make a note of that, Clerk!' said the Judge quickly.

Next morning as the actors came into the café, Licenciado Ruelas called them over one by one to introduce them to us. With them was Armando Oliverez Carillo, who had taken the part of Cervantes when the plays were first produced.

'He was a magnificent Cervantes!' exclaimed Licenciado Ruelas when he had left. 'He would go to a hilltop above the town and practise with his cape, sweeping it round him superbly. Unfortunately when he became Federal Judge for Guanajuato he could no longer be in the plays.'

The actors were from all walks of life, from Professors of Languages, to lawyers, housewives and students.

'You must meet our Wardrobe Mistress! Come here a minute Chatta,' he called to a dark buxom young woman in a lace blouse. 'And here comes our present Cervantes—Lopez Saurez.' He beckoned to a young man in a check shirt. 'He has played the part one hundred and twenty times in the last six years. He will make a good Spaniard for us at the *hacienda* . . . and I think I know the very person for your *hacendado*' he added, 'and here he comes. Antonio Corona,' he called, beckoning to the dark young man who had been the resourceful Judge of last night.

Antonio Corona was more than willing to be our *hacendado*.

'Tonight I am playing an idiot in rags,' he exclaimed 'in the morning I shall be a *hacendado* in velvet! What could an actor ask more?'

By lunch time we had appointed not only our *hacendado*, but his wife, an overseer, servants, a sister from Spain and a dozen other mythical characters. It was arranged that we would meet in the Plaza de San Roque that afternoon to shoot the first scenes.

'What delightful people they are!' exclaimed Bill as one after the other they went off after shaking hands with us again.

Licenciado Ruelas smiled. 'We are like one large family here in Guanajuato. I think that is why we all love to be here!'

That afternoon in the Plaza de San Roque we found Chatta setting up her Wardrobe Room in one of the houses, and one by one the actors arrived with their costumes.

'Antonio Corona, you and Josefina will first play the part of a family of Guanajuato of today . . . Joya,' Licenciado Ruelas beckoned to his pretty niece, 'you will be their young daughter . . .' Soon the little square held a typical representation of everyday Mexican life. Even a policeman passing through was persuaded to join in, as well as an ice-cream seller and a vendor of *chicharron* (pork crackling).

Then came the transformation. We were standing on the same spot but three hundred years back in time. Instead of the typical Mexican family—the man in his check shirt and straw hat—there stood a Spanish *hacendado* in velvet breeches and doublet, with a sweeping feather in his cap. His wife was regal in black satin, their daughter in rose silk; instead of the khaki-clad policeman with his whistle, a watchman in a black cape patrolled the square with a staff. Two barefooted little Indians in *zarapes* had taken the place of the two schoolboys in shorts who had been playing *lotería* on the steps of the fountain and a cowled Franciscan monk was coming down the steps from the old church.

'Splendid!' exclaimed William.

The sun beat down, the costumes were extremely hot, and there was a constant shout from William of '*Otra vez!*' (Another time!) followed by a cry of '*Listos!* (Ready!) . . . *Cámara!* . . . *Acción!*' from Licenciado Ruelas. During every interlude the ice-cream man, who had really only stayed out of curiosity, found himself besieged by cavaliers and ladies, not to mention a monk and a nun.

During the week I got to know Guanajuato well for when we were not shooting scenes, I spent hours wandering up and down the steep alleys with their wrought-iron balconies full of plants. Between them lay little odd-shaped plazas with dripping fountains; above them, almost vertically, rose the pink hillsides that enclosed the town. There was something about Guanajuato that had attracted me instantly. (As a child I remember I once asked an elderly aunt, who seemed to know more than most people, why one liked some people at once and others not at all. Her reply was 'It all depends if your auras agree'. I had no idea what an aura was in those days, but I know now that she was quite correct, and I am sure it also applies to places.)

In the indoor market where fruit and vegetables made a sea of colour, an old wooden staircase led up to an encircling gallery where the floor was lined with pottery at ridiculous prices— huge ginger coloured *cazuelas* for only a few *pesos*; hand-made cups and saucers for fifty *centavos* each.

I discovered a plaque on the wall of one shabby house in Calle Positos which said that Diego Rivera had been born there on the 17th December 1886. It was now a dilapidated tenement building with peeling walls, but in the hallway was a cracked ornamental basin decorated with three dolphins and a dog's head which I am sure must have been a source of deep interest to the tiny Diego Rivera.

Just round the corner the new University of Guanajuato, with its magnificent flight of white steps, somehow managed to blend in perfectly with the sixteenth-century houses in between which it was snugly fitted.

But no matter which way I went there was one thing always in view since it stood high up on a hilltop overlooking the town. It was the statue of the young miner, Joseph Barajas (known as '*El Pipila*'), one of the Heroes of the Independence, who, with his blazing torch had set fire to the fort-like granary in which the Royalists had barricaded themselves. From the hooks still on its walls, the heads of Father Hidalgo and other Revolutionary leaders had been hung in 1811 as an example to the people.

One evening, not content with always seeing the statue from a distance, I set out to get a closer view. By taking the first alley I came to, and always climbing upwards, I found myself eventually right above the town at the very feet of '*El Pipila*'. Thirty feet high, and made of oblong pink stones, he towered over me, each of his finger nails about the size of my hand. At his feet was engraved the challenging inscription, '*Aun hay otras alhondigas por incendiar*' (There are still other castles to burn).

Next morning we set out for our first day's filming at the *hacienda*. Licenciado Ruelas and Chatta went ahead with a car full of costumes and props, while we followed with about fifteen people squeezed into the station wagon. By the time we arrived a room leading off the patio had already been turned into a Wardrobe Room and Chatta was laying out costumes, *zarapes* and swords on a huge canopied bed.

Those were wonderful days in the gardens of the *hacienda*, though it must have been terribly hot for the actors in those costumes. Yet not one of them ever complained, though they had their own play to do every evening; in fact I could never speak highly enough about their cheerfulness and friendly co-operation. In between scenes they would stretch out on the grass in the shade of the huge cypress trees or tuck up their silks and velvets and dangle their feet in the swimming pool. During one scene the wife of the *hacendado* and the sister from Spain sat doing some embroidery by a fountain, while the monk read aloud to them from a priceless sixteenth-century manuscript kindly lent by the real owners of the *hacienda*. I suddenly spotted five straw hats and five pairs of dark eyes over the top of a nearby hedge; it was the gardeners, staring in frank amazement at these 'ghosts' from the past. Indeed, costumes and setting fitted each other so perfectly (as they could hardly help doing) that I sometimes found it difficult to remember what century I *was* in.

Our last scene at the *hacienda* was the visit of the 'Spanish Viceroy', and the Ball. Our Viceroy was Ernesto Scheffler, and it was not till we were sharing a stone step together between scenes that I discovered he was the Director of Philosophy at the University.

The Ball was held on the patio with our 'minstrels' gathered at one end playing a sedate waltz. 'One, two, three' mouthed Licenciado Ruelas from behind William and the cameras, as costumed figures bowed, smiled and turned, gracefully and politely. There was a pause for a moment while Bill inserted a new reel of film. Instantly the 'minstrels' broke out into a hot Cuban rhythm, the sedate ladies tucked up their velvet skirts and began to 'Rock and Roll' and the *hacendado* seized the Wardrobe Mistress and whirled her round in a wild polka. The whole patio became alive with noise and laughter.

'*Otra Vez!*' shouted William. '*Listos ... Cámara ... Acción!*' called Licenciado Ruelas. At once it became again a sedate scene of politely bowing cavaliers and ladies.

After the Ball the 'Viceroy' and his party were shown being served with hot chocolate in gold-rimmed cups, for the Spaniards had taken avidly to the Aztec drink. Servants would bring hot chocolate to their mistresses during Mass, until such an orgy of chocolate drinking went on in church—not only among the congregation but also among the clergy—that at last the Pope forbade it. One Bishop was excommunicated for refusing to give it up, while a Dominican friar was poisoned by it—which led to the Mexican expression, 'to give him his chocolate'.

Actually it was an extremely potent beverage then, for the Aztec way of making it was to crush and beat up the *cacao* beans in a little water, remove the oily skum—which was added again later—mix the remainder with maize dough, and heat it. When cool it was seasoned with herbs, chile and honey, whipped up, and then poured from a height into a gourd bowl. Because it had a slightly bitter flavour the Aztecs called it *xocolatl*, from *xococ* (bitter) and *atl* (water). The nearest the Spaniards could get to that was 'chocolate'.

At the end of the patio behind huge double doors was the private chapel of the *hacienda*. Its altar, entirely of gold panels, had been brought over from Spain. It made a perfect setting for our final 'shot'—the *hacendado* and his wife kneeling there together with the monk in his rough brown habit on the altar steps.

As we drove home from the *hacienda* that day the actors pointed out the square-topped crag called the Buff. A pilgrimage is made on the feast of Saint Ignacio to a shrine on its summit, with picnics, and, of course, plenty to drink. Since it is in July when it always rains, some students of Guanajuato made a good profit one year by running a car with the announcement, 'We take care of a drunken man! One *peso* if fighting; fifty *centavos* if insensible.'

In the streets of Guanajuato we were held up by a long procession of men carrying sheaves of gladioli.

'This is the time when all the workers take flowers to the Virgin of Guanajuato,' explained Licenciado Ruelas. 'Today it is the electric light workers; tomorrow the telephone workers and Sunday, the miners.'

The streets were also full of tiny white-clad children carrying flowers. I followed some of them into a church and found an enormous cardboard 'M', perforated with holes, propped up on the altar steps. Children were running up the aisles with a single flower, sticking it in one of the holes, then running back to fetch another from their mothers who sat with a bunch on their laps handing out one at a time. It was like some lovely party game with tiny figures running delightedly up and down the aisles, laughing and chattering. The result was a gigantic flowered 'M'.

Next morning we set out to 'shoot' the Indian life sequence. The owner of a small *adobe* house set on a stony hillside was delighted to hire out his home to us for the day. Five or six donkeys which had just been let loose rushed up to a dust-filled hollow and rolled over and over in it kicking their legs up in a cloud of dust. They looked happy enough but there were many sores on their backs from the wooden saddles and heavy packs.

The owner of the house, his wife and six children were living in a tiny *adobe* structure composed of two windowless rooms; the furniture was an old bedstead, several rolled-up *petate* mats, a shabby wooden chest for clothes, and two orange boxes.

While kneeling figures dressed as Indians of the sixteenth century got busy with *tortilla*-making in the dusty yard, I was invited indoors by the wife who pulled the two orange boxes across to the doorway so that she and I could sit in the shade yet watch what was going on. She, her husband, the baby and three of the children slept in this room. The adjoining room was filled to half-way up the walls with a great heap of maize cobs and on these were spread two *petate* mats to serve as beds for the older boys.

The mother looked lovingly at the baby asleep in her *rebozo*.

'When he is one year old,' she said, 'he will not have milk any more but will have two *tortillas* every day.'

She told me that she made *atole* for the children and for her husband to take to the fields by boiling up the maize dough with water. This makes a very nourishing drink. Along with the twenty-five *tortillas* she made every day for her husband to take to the fields she also made ten for the dog.

It was now time for Antonio Corona, as *hacendado*, to inspect the cattle. For this the Professor of Languages, who was taking the part of our *peón* had to round up the cows which were scattered about the maize field.

'Oh, but he's got his shoes on!' shouted someone. The poor Professor, having removed the offending items, walked gingerly across the rough stubble on his bare feet. As Antonio Corona appeared on the scene in scarlet velvet (as a Spaniard *he* was allowed to keep his shoes on) one of the cows turned and nuzzled him gently with its horns. Antonio backed away. '*Hacendado!*' he exclaimed indignantly to William. 'No bullfighter!'

Getting 'shots' of the ploughing of the maize field by our *peón* was even more complicated. Two cows, yoked together, were attached by a chain to the wooden plough; the Professor had to guide this with one hand and manipulate the eight-foot goad with the other. It looked simple, but he could not get the wooden furrow to stay in the ground; it careered about wildly in front of his bare feet. The cows, upset by this unfamiliar display of temperament, broke into a trot and began careering across the field taking plough and Professor with them. Clearly he could not learn the art in a morning; something different must be thought of. It was Licenciado Ruelas, as resourceful as ever, who solved the problem. While the real *peón*, having quietened down his team, obligingly turned them round and ploughed a couple of furrows, his facial expressions and hand movements were carefully noted; then the cows were detached leaving the plough still in the ground. The Professor and the *peón* changed places, and with one hand on the plough handle and the other grasping the goad, he prodded an imaginary team and 'wrestled' with the stationary plough encouraged by remarks like 'Imagine you've just hit a stone!' . . . 'Look as if it's harder work!'

That evening when we got back to Guanajuato we found a group of men gathered round a huge conical framework of sticks, about thirty feet high, which lay sprawled across the centre of the square. It was a *castillo* (a Castle of fireworks) and was part of the celebrations for the four hundredth Anniversary of the Naming of the Virgin of Guanajuato. It was exciting to watch it being lit that evening. Little figures lit up and exploded one by one, seeming to jump off the *castillo* and into the air.

Cortés had brought gunpowder to Mexico; when he ran out of it, he had made his own from charcoal, nitrate salt, and sulphur —daringly scraped from the very walls of the crater of Popocatépetl. At first it was magic to the Indians, but they soon discovered how to make it for themselves and before long fireworks had become as much a part of their religious ceremonies as holy water or incense. Now, every holiday in Mexico, religious or civic, is celebrated with fireworks as a matter of course, and the 15th September, the Day of Independence, is the noisiest day in Mexico.

Nearly all the fireworks are made in little home 'factories', of which there are over four thousand in the State of Mexico; in fact, the thing became so dangerous that it is now forbidden to make, or let off, fireworks in Mexico City itself.

The next location on our script was the silver mine from which our *hacendado* had obtained his wealth. Loaded down with actors and props we drove up into the hills above Guanajuato to a tiny silver-mining village. Here we left the station wagon and were taken by lorry up an almost vertical mountain track to the mine— a tunnel going right into the mountainside. After Chatta had finished in her impromptu Wardrobe Room between the truck and a wall of rock, we set off in an incongruous procession, and were soon swallowed up in the dark dank interior which, after the blazing heat outside, seemed icily cold. Finally we reached a fork in the tunnel which would serve as a base. Here William and Bill set up spotlights and cameras and work began. The half naked 'Indians' had the baskets on their backs secured by straps round their heads in the correct Aztec manner. At intervals we all crouched against the dripping walls to let a string of trucks filled with ore go rumbling by.

I went off to do some exploring on my own, and found that the fork in the tunnel led directly to an opening into the wall of the great shaft, one of the deepest silver mine shafts in the world. A helmeted miner was on guard at the small iron platform which jutted out into the shaft. By standing on this platform I could see a round patch of blue sky high above me where the shaft began; below I looked down into depth upon depth of what would ordinarily have been a dark well over a thousand feet deep. But it so happened (how lucky can you be?) that this was the one day in the year when the sun passes directly over the shaft at midday— and it was exactly midday.

I found myself looking down, not into darkness, but into a seemingly endless tube of gold and silver and multi-coloured light. Grey ferns, growing out of the wet rock walls and hung with dew drops, were being spun into rainbows. The walls themselves appeared to be smoking which gave the whole thing an ethereal effect. It was so hypnotizingly beautiful that I leaned over the rail still further. Like most moments of intense beauty it was transient. At that moment the guard grabbed my arm and pulled me back. The dark shape of an empty truck came bearing down upon us almost brushing the platform on which we stood. A small shower of broken rock clattered down to fall with a plop far below. By the time I looked down again the sun had passed the zenith and there was nothing to see.

From behind me in the tunnel came the familiar shouts of *'Otra vez . . . Listos . . . Camára . . . Accíon!'*

When we finally emerged again into the hot sun my dress clung as damply and as coldly against my legs as if it had been dipped in iced water.

Down in the tiny mining village we found one of the most elaborate and beautiful churches in *churrigueresca* style, its brownish-pink stone façade entirely covered with tiny carved figures. Inside, though rather gloomy, it was fascinating because rear and side walls were hung with *retablos* (miracle paintings). Painted on wood, canvas or metal they depicted 'miraculous' escapes or recoveries which the donors and their families had experienced. Mostly they were incidents in the mine—lurid scenes of breaking cables; of figures crumpled up at the bottom of shafts; of tunnels blocked by débris. One painting showed a flock of goats before and after foot and mouth disease, another, a woman lying in bed, and a crude picture of a car knocking her down. Among the paintings hung wooden legs, X-ray plates threaded on a piece of string, crutches, a torn shirt worn during an accident, even a whole plaster.

'Some have been here for two or three hundred years,' said Licenciado Ruelas. 'In all towns in Mexico you will find an artist who makes such *retablos*; often he is also a potter or a weaver.

When somebody has a "miraculous" escape, they visit him and tell him and commission him to paint it.'

In addition there were the usual collection of little *milagros* (silver tokens), this time pinned on to a flannel apron tied round a statue.

Down in the town of Guanajuato there was a memorial to the miners. From inside a great rock, on which stood a fine sculpture of a miner with his pick, protruded two little rails holding an identical truck to the ones which had rumbled past us that morning in the tunnel. It was filled with ore among which were several glittering specimens containing real specks of silver and gold. Like most people, I suppose, I tried to pick one up to examine it—and found it was firmly glued in.

It was while I was looking at this, that I became aware of a thin tapping sound coming from the cave-like interior of a tiny workshop in one of the tall narrow houses. A shaft of moted sunlight glinted on gold and silver, as an old man, glasses on the end of his nose, tapped away at something resting on a worn block of wood. Beside him on the table lay a dusty heap of the little *milagros*. It was rather like standing on the threshold of the cave of the Rhinegold dwarfs. Sensing that someone was watching him he pushed his glasses back on his nose, and looked up.

'*Adios, señorita!*' he exclaimed with a smile and a nod (I could never quite get used to the way *adios* could mean either Hallo or Goodbye). He told me that he had been making these little tokens for nearly sixty years. Picking up a handful of hearts, legs, pigs, horses and dogs, he blew the dust off them and tipped them into my palm for inspection. They were beautifully made and I complimented him on his work.

'Ah!' he said regretfully, 'but once they were made only of good silver, señorita. Now it is just alloy, for they must be so cheap that even the poorest can buy them.'

At last the night came for which I had been waiting—the repeat performance of the *Entremesses* of Cervantes. Though we had seen a different play every night, I wanted so much to see once more that first scene which had made such an impression on me.

Unfortunately it was also the last night of the Plays, and, for us, the last night in Guanajuato. William was giving a party for all the actors at our hotel after the performance and we were leaving in the morning.

We were already on our way to the Plaza de San Roque when I discovered that I had left the key of my room in the door.

'You go on and I'll catch you up,' I said to William and Bill and hurried back to the hotel. By the time I arrived at the plaza it was already in darkness; I slipped quietly behind the crowded stands into the empty side alley and sat down on the edge of the pavement. Out of the darkness came the soft strains of two horns and a flute—the *Entremesses* had begun.

An old night watchman with a flaming torch came and lighted the nine lanterns around the old stone cross in the centre of the square; above in the belfrey, the bells, caught ghostly white in a spotlight, began to move, gently at first, then clamouring into the night. As the sound died into silence, from somewhere level with the rooftops came the voice of Licenciado Ruelas just as I remembered it on that first night—but now it was such a familiar voice, and now it was the Prologue.

'. . . This is the imaginary world of Cervantes, and the reality of his world . . . The bells are ringing sweet on the night air . . . the tongue of the bells, born of a Spanish genius, Don Miguel de Cervantes, bells of the earth by his glory swinging . . .'

Like the Epilogue, the Prologue had been written by Armando Oliverez Carillo—'that magnificent Cervantes' who had become a Federal Judge. (What did it feel like, I wondered, to be a Federal Judge when you had once been Cervantes? Could it ever satisfy you?)

Soft footsteps sounded in the alley. I turned my head, but it was too dark; I could see no one. Then the spotlight swung across the square and I saw Cervantes standing not five feet away. He walked past me and on into the square, his eyes grave, his cloak wrapped round him, deep in thought. At the same time, into the square from all sides came the people, the everyday people, who were to be immortalized by his pen—the peasants, the housewives, the soldiers. . . . He walked unnoticed amongst them as they jostled each other in the square. Mounting the steps to the church, he stood leaning against the stone balustrade, his eyes following their every movement—*his* players . . . *his* characters . . . . . . *his* world-to-be.

One by one the spotlights picked them out . . . the old beggar in his rags; the soldier who had drunk too well . . . the wife nagging her husband . . . the gipsy girl with her beribboned tambourine.

A shadow moved along the wall of the church. Cervantes descended again into the square and vanished into the darkness.

And now, one by one, the short allegorical sketches were enacted, beginning with the man who thought he was made of glass and ran away from everyone crying, 'Don't touch me! You'll break me!' Finally came the last sketch in which a whole town is deluded by two unscrupulous characters into the belief that the ground is covered with rats. Stamping, shouting, crying, the inhabitants fought first with the imaginary rats, then with each other, till at last the square was, as I remembered it on that first night, a tableau of desolation strewn with still bodies. This time, however, I realized what it meant, that it symbolized the narrow vision of humanity which, as yet, does not see beyond death or destruction.

Now, once again there came a spotlight in a dark alleyway and the flash from the red silk lining of a cloak—which I knew now to be caused by no chance drift of wind but a well-timed gesture, once rehearsed to perfection on a hilltop. Once again I watched the tall black-robed figure thread his way between the bodies on the ground; then, his shadow growing longer before him on the cobbles, he disappeared into the darkness.

A moment of silence, then the Epilogue I remembered so well . . .

'As his shadow is lost in the shadow of the street, his life gone from the history of men, Cervantes is born into the second and the true life . . .'

With a clatter of hooves two figures, one on a horse, the other on a donkey, came riding down into the square. The deep voice from the darkness continued . . . 'King of Gentlemen, Lord of the Sad . . . you who take glory and dress it with dreams . . . crowned with a golden Helmet of Illusions . . . never yet defeated . . . the shield on your armour, fantasy . . . and your lance all hot . . .' and Don Quixote followed his creator into immortality.

The applause was tumultuous, the audience calling out for Licenciado Ruelas, cheering him as he descended from his improvised rostrum on one of the rooftops. Everyone gathered round him, all trying to shake his hand at once. He made a short speech, but before we could applaud there came a loud bray from the donkey—'The first time in all the years that he has brayed at this moment!' exclaimed Licenciado Ruelas when the laughter had died down.

Back at the *posada* a table had been spread with a fine buffet supper for William's farewell party, and the room was soon filled to overflowing with actors and their friends. The whole room stood up and cheered as Licenciado Ruelas entered, ending with repeated shouts of 'Ruelas! Ruelas! Ra Ra Ra!' Then a host of glasses were raised to William, Bill and myself with cries of '*Salud! Salud!*'

I remembered the words of Licenciado Ruelas on that first morning in the little café—'We are like one happy family here in Guanajuato!' How abundantly that had been demonstrated to us —and how generously and spontaneously we ourselves had been included in it. Sad, indeed, to think that this time tomorrow we should be far away from Guanajuato.

CHAPTER 14

THE RAINY SEASON; NOGALES AND
MONTE ALBAN

WITH JUNE the rainy season arrived. I would wake as usual to brilliant sunshine, but every day, at about one o'clock, dark clouds would pile up, thunder would rumble from the mountains beyond the Pedregal, and the next moment rain would be flooding down. Within minutes you would step off the kerb into water over your ankles as the narrow streets of San Angel became small rushing torrents. The downpour sometimes lasted a couple of hours. Then the rain ceased as abruptly as it had begun, the sun broke through, and the sky became cloudless again; in the small plazas the dripping trees smelt delicious and the dust was well and truly laid.

It was never wise to go out without a raincoat now since you could not rely on the rain coming at the same time each day—it might be earlier or later. I remember being on a packed second-class bus in Insurgentes in the midday rush-hour just as the rain began. The cascade of water was so violent that the windscreen-wipers (never too reliable at the best of times on a second-class bus) were knocked out of action instantly. However, this did not deter the driver, who began to charge blindly through rain and traffic, trusting, no doubt, to the many holy pictures on his windscreen to clear the way. Twice we swerved to a screeching standstill which sent those of us who were packed down the aisle tumbling headfirst on top of each other; next moment, with horns hooting furiously all round us, we were skidding the whole width of the road and back again to the screaming of wet brakes. By this time the driver's face was streaming with perspiration,

[179]

as much from fear as from the heat, and his eyes had a hunted expression since he could see nothing at all through the curtain of water that surrounded us. As for us, his passengers, we hardly knew whether it was better to continue in this perilous fashion all the way to San Angel, or to get out while we could, and be drenched from head to foot within seconds; added to which as it was the rush-hour every succeeding bus, trolley and *peso* taxi would be packed. One or two, deciding to risk their fate by water, leapt off knee-deep into it at the next traffic lights, and were instantly swallowed up in the deluge. Seeing this the rest of us decided to stay where we were. Eventually we did reach San Angel, and there we, in our turn, descended into the swirling waters, most of the passengers with their shoes in their hands.

One morning I heard a familiar voice on the telephone; it was William Deneen.

'Hallo! I just thought I'd ring up to tell you Bill and I are leaving for Detroit in a couple of days' time. I suppose we can't give you a lift anywhere on the way? We shall be crossing the Mexican border at Matamoros.'

I had no idea where Matamoros was, but at any rate it was a different part of the border from Laredo. Snap decisions seemed to be my fate where William and Bill were concerned—I remembered that ten-second one at San Cristóbal.

'Lovely!' I said. 'I'll come to Matamoros' and then went to look at my map to see where it was.

I found that it was the easternmost point of entry into Mexico from the States, and a pleasing idea occurred to me. If I could find my way across the States to Arizona I could then re-enter Mexico at Nogales, the westernmost point of entry; from there I could probably get a bus going down the west coast and get back to Mexico City that way. I went immediately to the bus station to buy a ticket in advance so that I would not have to carry much money with me.

'No, what I want to do . . .' I began for the fourth time (it was difficult enough to explain it in English let alone in Spanish), 'is to cross over *here*, and then somehow get to *there* so that I can

Margarita Urueta looking at the portrait of her father, Jesús Urueta, in Chihuahua University

'We shall have like him our spirit filled with hope and our eyes fixed on the stars . . .'. Mural in Chihuahua University symbolizing the future of Mexico

Young Mexican weaver at the *rebozo* school, Santa Maria del Rio

The new University of Guanajuato fits perfectly into its sixteenth-century setting

cross back again and come back to Mexico City by the west coast
—but be able to get off the bus for a few days anywhere I like.'

The official found the whole thing incomprehensible. Why go
all the way up to the east to get to the west? Why not just go up
the west coast? I tried to explain that leaving Mexico at the easternmost point and re-entering it at the westernmost point had a
peculiar attraction for me, but this was beyond him altogether.
Finally, after much biting of his pen, he made out a ticket assuring
me that with that I could get on and off every bus on the West
Coast.

It was over six hundred miles to Matamoros and even though
the rainy season was in operation in the south, the road from San
Luis Potosí to Monterrey was just a white-hot desert where only
little clouds of dust indicated a wandering flock of goats, or one
sheep and one goat tied together by a rope at the neck. Yucca
trees, which in January had been just gaunt spiky bushes, now
each held a huge single plume of white blossom that bubbled
down the stem like froth.

By the second evening the mountains of Monterrey, ribbed
into a rugged richness, smoothed into sinuous seams, dominated
all the landscape. The heat was so tremendous now that, to avoid
it, we left Monterrey at three o'clock in the morning, yet already
the air was like a furnace and blocks of ice were already being
delivered in the streets.

As we drove due east the whole windscreen was transformed
into a wide Technicolor screen by the sunrise. It was a rough road
to Matamoros, still unmade in places, sometimes deviating over
fields, so that several times we had to stop and look at the map,
not at all sure if we were still on the route. Small townships were
just wooden shacks set down in the scrub along an earth street,
and by seven o'clock people were already out with hoses spraying
the street in an effort to keep down the dust. Once we met a
yellow cart rattling along; the young woman driving it, her long
hair streaming out in the hot wind, was handling her team of four
mules like an old hand.

There were now fields of what I took to be runner beans; but soon they stretched away into the horizon on either side of the road. I knew Mexicans went in for beans in a big way but somehow I had not associated them with runner beans to this extent. Later I found they were cotton fields, and I remembered the words of the Patrol Officer at Laredo when he had talked about the banks of the Rio Grande . . . 'soft as face powder, anything grows. You can put a crop of cotton in and it'll come up . . .' Judging by the amount surrounding us, it didn't do too badly here either.

At Matamoros, a ramshackle border town of shabby wooden houses and dusty streets, we crossed the International Bridge, over what is the Rio Brava on the Mexican side and the Rio Grande on the other, and found ourselves in Brownsville, Texas.

I now made my way by devious ways, chiefly Greyhound bus, across the States to Arizona, and in due course found myself in Nogales. There was no river to mark the border here, simply a high wire fence that divided the streets and then zigzagged its way up and over the hillsides.

A bus was leaving next morning for Mexico City and I boarded it looking forward to enjoying a few days here, there and anywhere all down the west coast, but when I explained to the driver what I was going to do he shook his head.

'No, señorita. Impossible with this ticket. This is a ticket only for one bus—from Nogales to Mexico City.'

'But it doesn't stay anywhere long enough for me to *see* anything,' I protested. 'They told me in Mexico City . . .'

He shrugged. 'No, señorita. When you leave my bus I must take this ticket. But you need not use this ticket—you can buy other tickets. They will give you your money back in Mexico City.'

It was check-mate! I had bought the ticket in advance in order *not* to have much money on me; I could *not* buy more tickets.

But for all that it turned out to have its compensations. I had a window-seat and for most of that one thousand five hundred-mile journey the road ran along beside the coast, and I have never before, or since, seen such sunsets. Beginning as feathers and wings and all things ethereal, they would deepen through every shade of rose into a single sheet of crimson to encompass the entire western horizon and the whole sea itself. As for the nights, and there were three of them, it was full moon, and of such a brilliance that I could not bear to waste them in sleep, but sat all night in the dark bus watching the silver panorama sliding by. When I think of that road from Nogales now I see it not as places, only as alternations of sunset and moonlight.

Much had happened in San Angel during my absence. Margarita had found the French poodle running frenziedly round and round the garden one morning. She and Marta had caught him and shut him up indoors and then sent for the vet, who had diagnosed rabies and ordered him to be destroyed immediately. Now both Margarita and Marta were having to have a twenty-day course of anti-rabies injections since they had both been well licked by the poodle. (Because of the fear of rabies you seldom see anyone in Mexico patting a stray dog.)

For months now I had been intending to go back to Oaxaca to see the ruins of Monte Albán and Mitla.

'But you *must* see Monte Albán in the early morning light!' someone said to me one day, with such fervour that I resolved that that was exactly what I would do. Since the rains, the whole Valley of Mexico would be green—that was something I badly wanted to see too.

I found that a train was leaving Mexico City at four o'clock that evening; by travelling all night I could be in Oaxaca about six next morning. (How I would get out to Monte Albán at that time I had no idea, but I was prepared to work that out when I got there.)

The train turned out to be a First Class Pullman—a luxurious affair with blue carpets and padded seats; for thirty *pesos* extra I could also have a bed.

As we left the city behind I watched eagerly to see the change made by the rains. It was certainly startling, as if someone had splashed green paint over a grey canvas. Where before two figures would be walking down a field path in a small cloud of dust, now they walked ankle-deep in a rich greenness; where, by contrast to the parched earth, the *maguey* had looked positively green, now, because of the vividness of meadow and maize, it looked merely grey-blue. Everywhere I looked there was water—in furrows, in ditches, in lagoons—and cows grazed contentedly on grass instead of dust. Pepper trees were smothered in tiny lemon coloured flowers; the flowers round the discs of the *nopal* cactus had turned into rose-red *tuna* plums; and fields of mustard were caught up like a yellow sash between mauve mountains.

When the white-coated attendant came round to make up the beds, there were so few people on the train that I could choose where I wanted to sleep. I was glad of that—I wanted a lower berth that was all window on the side of the sunrise. I got it, complete with clean sheets and heavy green curtains that shut out the rest of the carriage. It was quite the most luxurious travelling I had done in Mexico. I appreciated it even more when we stopped to let the second-class train for Mexico City go past. From my comfortable bed I could see the passengers sitting bolt upright packed together amidst a confusion of baskets and bundles.

At about half-past four I awoke to see a clear-cut wedge of stars knifed in between two mountain peaks. We were making our way with some difficulty through steep precipitous gorges and thick jungle, and our tiny single-line railway looked like a child's toy. As the stars paled, threads of pink began to pick out the east, deepening into clear rose. I could think of nothing nicer than being alone to watch the dawn break over those jungled gorges—yet, at the same time, most comfortably in bed.

Soon I could define patches of cultivation, minute red clearings on some craggy hillside representing heaven knows how many months of hard work with a digging stick; as it grew lighter I could make out the white coats and cotton trousers of Indians already at work on their *milpas* while it was still cool. We were now in the rich valleys of Oaxaca, rich not only in soil and vegetation, but in their wealth of archeological sites, for over two hundred have been discovered here, though only three—Monte Albán, Mitla, and Yagul—have been partly reconstructed.

When we reached Oaxaca it was still so early that the sun was barely up. The porter on the station told me there was only one

way to get to Monte Albán and that was by taxi. In the *zocalo* two
or three were parked under the huge Indian laurels I remembered
so well; spotting a potential customer, the drivers, as one, started
up their engines and swerved across. I picked the one with the
nicest face, jumped in, and said: 'I want to go to Monte Albán,
please—but I want to get there quickly.' He looked a little surprised that anyone should want to go to Monte Albán at that
time of the morning, let alone quickly, but obligingly skidded
round the *zocalo* on two wheels and began to race through the
narrow streets.

Once in the open country, we began to climb by a steep winding road till the town lay far below us, hidden by wreaths of early
morning mist. At the top we pulled up under a big tree overhanging the valley, and within minutes, I found myself standing
at the entrance to the Grand Plaza of Monte Albán just as the
early morning light was touching it into glory. It was an enormous rectangle surrounded by flat-topped pyramids, yet the first
impact on me was not one of awe, as at Teotihuacán where the
massive Pyramid of the Sun dominates the whole scene. It lay
rather in the quiet rhythm of composition whereby each pyramid
seemed to subordinate itself to the perfection of the whole, like
the petals of a flower. A chain of smoky-blue mountains encircled
the site, yet distant enough and below it, so that they did not
close it in but merely formed an outer fringe of beauty, like the
green frill round an aconite. The steep sides of the pyramids had
once been covered with coloured stucco, but, for their main effect,
the ancient Zapotec architects of Monte Albán had relied upon
the ever-changing interplay of light, for this hilltop arena is a
focal point for the sun from its rising to its setting.

My Zapotec taxi-driver, delighted at my reaction to this masterpiece of his ancestors, was only too willing to share with me all
he knew of its past. He pointed out how the ancient builders had
transformed the natural features of the hilltop by levelling and
hewing away the outcrops of rock, or, if they could not do this,
crowning them with a structure to hide them, so that the core of
many a pyramid was just natural rock. The result was, however,

that the two great stairways of the north and south pyramids finished up a little askew, while not all the mounds lie strictly along the axis of the plaza. The Zapotecs of a later period, anxious to hide this discrepancy on the part of their predecessors, added a couple of small structures and created an optical illusion bringing the whole thing into alignment.

As far as archeologists know man first appeared at Monte Albán between 700 and 300 B.C.; in the Building of the Dancers I saw slabs dating back to 500 B.C. which were carved not only with figures of dancers but with glyphs and numerical signs, showing that a calendar and a system of writing was in use even then. Then, towards the end of the tenth century, Monte Albán was suddenly and mysteriously abandoned, or rather, turned into a huge burial-ground, for there are spectacular tombs all along the hillside.

In Tombs Nos. 104 and 105 the walls are covered in paintings. It is even possible to tell the Calendar names of the people by their head-dresses; for instance one woman is wearing a head-dress like a tiger; her Calendar name is 4 Tiger. The figures, nine male and nine female, are believed to represent the nine Gods of Death and their respective wives.

The most exciting discovery of all was the one made by Dr. Alfonso Caso in Tomb No. 7. This tomb already had a Zapotec occupant, but about the middle of the fourteenth century he was joined by an important Mixtec chief (for the Mixtecs had by then over-run the Valley of Oaxaca), and with *him* was buried an absolute hoard of gold, silver, alabaster, jade and turquoise—the most important treasure ever discovered in America.

'All those things are now in Oaxaca in our Museum,' said the taxi-driver proudly.

That evening, back in Oaxaca, I went in search of the Museum, and in a room leading off the pillared patio with its trailing ferns, I found the treasures of Tomb No. 7. They lay in glass cases— exquisite necklaces of filigree gold hung with gold droplets; earrings; pendants dripping with jade, turquoise and gold. . . . Alongside was a photograph of Dr. Caso on his hands and knees in the tomb examining the find during the first memorable moments.

Yagul was more of a problem to find as it lay up in the mountains between Oaxaca and Mitla, and a couple of miles off the road. However a little bus passed the cart track that led to it, and next day I set off on foot between tangled hedges of Morning Glory and flowering cactus. It was scorchingly hot in spite of billowing clouds; an Indian in white cotton trousers and straw hat was sitting in the shade of the hedge eating his breakfast of *tortillas*, his jug of *pulque* beside him. Once I met a cart—just a couple of planks fixed between two huge wooden wheels—drawn by a pair of white oxen, and had to scramble down into the ditch so that it could get past.

After about three-quarters of an hour, involving many detours through ditches and fields since the track had been badly flooded, I found myself at the foot of the mountain. On a low plateau half-way up I found the ruins of Yagul. There was a great Ball Court of magnificent proportions, and organ cactus, twenty feet high, reared up against the remnants of delicately carved walls in palace patios.

Later that day I found my way to Mitla, a tiny village of dusty streets. In an open space beyond stood a huge *mesquite* tree, and on either side of this lay two exquisite things: the sixteenth-century church, a group of delicate pink domes set against a background of smoke-blue ranges; and the Palaces of Mitla, fragile, compact and beautiful.

I wandered through tiny ruined quadrangles and chambers whose walls were covered in a mosaic-like pattern, so close and fine that at first I thought it was carved into the stone. (Actually the walls of mud and stone are inlaid with thousands of small sculptured stones of different shapes, hammered in one at a time to form numberless designs. Altogether there are over one hundred thousand of these shaped stones in the walls.) Many of the chambers were still roofless, and there the sunlight, gilding each fragment of the stone mosaic, produced an almost magical effect. As Mitla was still in use the Spaniards had torn down part of it and built a church on top, using the same stones, so right up against the back of the church are more patios with long lovely panellings of inlaid stone.

When I finally left Oaxaca I went to the station in good time to catch the nine o'clock train back to Mexico City, looking forward to another night in that comfortable berth. Guessing that there would be a *refresco* service on the Pullman I did not bother to buy even a banana (always safe) for the journey.

The station was already crowded though there was still half an hour before the train was due. The moustached official in the booking office shook his head. 'No sleeper tonight, señorita.'

For a moment I was taken aback. 'Oh well, just one single then,' I said, then, remembering that second-class train that had passed packed to suffocation, 'First Class, please.' He shook his head. 'No First Class tonight, señorita—Second Class only.' When I asked him to book me a seat on that he eyed me sadly. 'No reservations tonight—only tickets.'

Well, at least I had a ticket. I joined the throng on the packed platform and sat down on my haversack to wait. An hour and a half later the train ambled in. More by luck than judgment I got a seat. My companion was a burly Mexican with countless baskets of pottery which he had bought cheaply in Oaxaca and was hoping to dispose of profitably in Mexico City; in fact, the train was packed with people who had been buying things cheaply in Oaxaca to sell more profitably somewhere else. String bags, cardboard boxes, crates, pillowcases, all bulged with pottery. We looked like an overcrowded Christmas night.

When we finally got away at about half-past ten, many passengers began to play cards and a couple of guitarists settled down to a duet. The clink of bottles and the warm smell of *tortillas* being taken out of their cloth wrappings made me aware that I was hungry. As all the windows were wide open, mothers started to wind their *rebozos* round their babies to protect them against certain 'spirits of the air' of whom the Mexican Indians are particularly suspicious. When the guard lowered the lights a trifle snores began to rise and fall in every key. I put my feet up on

one of my companion's baskets of pottery, wedged my haversack against the window for a pillow, and was soon asleep too.

At three o'clock we were prodded awake by a small ticket
inspector; most tickets were found after a little sleepy fumbling
in pockets, the folds of *rebozos* or *zarapes*, or inside hat-bands, but
there was one man who had no ticket, and moreover refused
point-blank to pay for one. He was sprawled in the seat across the
aisle from me, had obviously had had rather a lot of *tequila*, and
was annoyed at being woken up for such a trifle.

No, he had no ticket. . . . Why should he have a ticket? . . . The
railways belonged to the Mexican people now . . . and with this
he turned his back on the little inspector and went to sleep again.

The inspector retired, apparently defeated, but in a few minutes
we heard the tramp of heavy feet, and two soldiers, in ill-fitting
tunics but with loaded rifles, came swaying up the coach; behind
them trotted the inspector. The soldiers clicked their heels and
stood to attention; the man was prodded awake again, and the
sight of two rifle butts level with his ears sobered him up mar-
vellously. Thrusting a hand inside his jacket he pulled out a wad of
pesos and threw them down on the seat. The inspector sorted out
the right money, laid the change on top politely, and wrote him
out a receipt. The soldiers turned on their heels and marched
away and we all settled down to sleep again.

Next morning as we emerged from a long pull through the
pine forests beyond Puebla the sun was just rising. There, snow-
capped and beautiful in its first rays, their slopes still ethereal with
mist, stood Popocatépetl and Ixtaccíhuatl. After that we never lost
sight of them for long. Sometimes they might seem to be lost as
we plunged into some cutting or forest, but next moment there
they were again, and more beautiful every time as the sun increased its gold and the shadows melted away from their slopes.
In fact it soon began to seem like some sort of a game in which we
were just going round and round them, for they kept appearing
first on one side of the train then on the other.

At every wayside station, often nothing more than a few
adobe huts, women in aprons and *rebozos* came rushing on to the

line, clamouring below the open windows, holding up their little wooden barrels of frothy white *pulque*—a chipped pottery mug dangling on each finger; others had flat pans of hot *tacos*, *enchilladas* dripping with sauce, or blue zinc pails of hot *tortillas*.

'*Quiere tortas?*' '*Quiere enchilladas?*' '*Quiere pulque?*' they would cry, running from one window to another, stuffing the dirty *peso* notes down the bibs of their aprons. Then the train would grind forward and they would merge back into the station again until it was time for the next one. The comings and goings of the few trains set the whole pattern of life for these tiny settlements alongside the railway.

I soon found that this train had one advantage over the luxurious Pullman with its hygienically sealed windows and air conditioning. Here one's head and shoulders could project from the wide open window, and since there was scarcely a foot of cinder track between us and the tall feathery maize or the blue-grey spears of *maguey*, and the train never got up much speed, it was as good as a stroll through the fields.

CHAPTER 15

CHIHUAHUA

THINGS must come to an end—but what a pity! Nearly eight months had passed since I had stood outside that gate in San Angel—wonderful months—and now it was time for me to be going back to England.

'Oh, I *am* going to miss you!' exclaimed Margarita, as we lingered over our breakfast trays. 'What a pity you have to go!' Then her face lit up. 'I know—I shall come with you as far as Chihuahua! The train to El Paso on the border passes right by it. Though my father was born in Chihuahua, I have never been there. I want to see his family house and the theatre where he gave his speech for Juárez, and the portrait of him at the University. Oh how nice!' Margarita's brown eyes sparkled. 'We will spend some days in Chihuahua and see all those things together!'

We went into town and bought our tickets well in advance to make sure we got a sleeper since Chihuahua is nearly two thousand miles from Mexico City and we would be two or three days on the train.

'I shall have a special farewell luncheon party for you that day,' said Margarita; 'all the family will come and afterwards we will ask many friends in for coffee. Then Pepe and Martita will drive us to the station to catch our train at seven o'clock. I shall tell Mina to pack up a fine parcel of food for us.'

At six o'clock on that last evening Margarita and I packed ourselves and my luggage into Pepe's car; the guests who still remained, clustered round to wave us farewell; from the open kitchen door came shouts of '*Perico, Perico!*' as the parrot, excited by all this activity, danced up and down in his cage.

It was sad to hear the huge iron gates clang behind me, to

thread through the dark familiar streets of San Angel and then
turn on to the brilliantly lighted avenue of Insurgentes, knowing
it was for the last time.

The train, scheduled to leave at seven, was still standing there at
eight; apparently the engine had not yet arrived. By nine o'clock
it had still not moved an inch either way. I have no idea what time
it did leave since we decided we might just as well get into our
berths and go to sleep. By the time we awoke in the morning we
were miles away from Mexico City.

For the next three days and nights we sat, slept and ate in the
train, for although we stopped frequently, often for no apparent
reason since there seemed no sign of habitation, we never stopped
anywhere long enough to do more than have a quick walk up
and down the small sun-scorched cinder track in order to stretch
our legs. However, there was a very good restaurant car, since
this was no local affair but the train to the border towns of Ciudad
Juárez and El Paso.

'What do you think happened coming up last time?' said a
woman sitting opposite. 'We were about an hour out of Mexico
City when the driver found he had left the conductor behind.
We had to go all the way back and pick him up!'

As we got further north we gradually left behind all traces of the
rich green which had sprung up in the Valley since the rainy
season. Once we left Zacatecas, a pink medieval fortress town set
down in a bare mountain valley, the empty spaces of the north
began to slide past monotonously. On either side the desert
stretched away to long mountains that could have been five, or
twenty-five, miles away, for the light was so luminous and
intense that one's sense of perspective became distorted.

At every tiny oven-hot station the train was besieged by sellers
of *zarapes*, *rebozos*, jewellery and leather handbags, all at prices
guaranteed to tempt any traveller just leaving the country to
fling discretion to the winds, and risk whatever might be involved in the way of Customs duty when he—or more likely she
—reached the border.

At last, however, on the third day the map showed that we

were nearing Chihuahua. My only link with it hitherto was that I associated it with the tiny elf-like dogs of the same name. Many people confuse the Chihuahua with the Mexican hairless dog, which appears on all the Diego Rivera murals in the National Palace; there are devoted adherents of the Chihuahua who claim that he and *not* the Mexican hairless was the one privileged to escort the soul over the river to its correct destination. However, once you see them side by side, you could never confuse them physically. Before I left England I had spent a day at the home of Colonel Vincent Harmer, Military Attaché in Mexico for several years. His wife, Hilary, had brought back with her several Mexican hairless dogs, and was the first person to breed them in England. The puppies were playing about on the lawn, their bare black skins as hot and dry to the touch as that of the adult dog, which were about the size of a plump fox terrier. With them were seven Chihuahuas, tiny things with pointed faces, prominent eyes and high-pitched barks. Even the fully grown ones were so minute that when Hilary held one up on the palm of her hand against a large dahlia blossom, the flower nearly eclipsed the dog; as for the Chihuahua puppies one of them sat comfortably inside a champagne glass.

The whole time I was in Chihuahua I did not see even one of these tiny dogs, though Hilary had told me that they *had* come across one village in the State of Chihuahua where small dogs, closely resembling Chihuahuas, had been sitting on many of the doorsteps; they had been told that, by tradition, households in that village had always had such little dogs.

Not far from Chihuahua station, rearing up on horseback above a pool of blue water, was the sculptured figure of Pancho Villa, the famous Mexican bandit and revolutionary, whose home had been in Chihuahua.

Our hotel overlooked the Cathedral square, and from the window we could see the pinky-fawn stone towers silhouetted against a background of dry gold plain rising to mauve mountain peaks. There were no suburbs to Chihuahua—it just was, then was not.

The house where Pancho Villa had lived was only a few streets away, a square pillared building standing right on the dusty pavement. His widow, motherly and plump, with tightly pulled back hair, and dressed all in black, showed us through the rooms which she had turned into a little museum in memory of him.

'I was born in the mountains here,' she said, 'and before I married Pancho I was a schoolteacher. The house is just as he arranged it for me.'

Her favourite picture of her husband in his wide bandit-like hat hung in the sitting room, alongside the rifle which he had used in the 1910 Revolution.

'You see, almost every Revolution in Mexico began up here,' explained Margarita, 'Chihuahua was the home, not only of Pancho Villa, the greatest revolutionary, but of the whole Revolution! All men who wanted to take arms against the Government came here because it was so near the United States border. Mexico was then so poor that there was no other possibility of a source of arms.'

Pancho Villa's real name had been Dorateo Aranga, but at sixteen, outlawed for the murder of a local tyrant, he adopted the name of the bandit of tradition, gathered a group of followers round him, and soon became a sort of Mexican Robin Hood, for though he plundered the rich ruthlessly he spared the poor out of sympathy. He and his men—who were known as the *Dorados* (the Golden Lads)—were feared all over Mexico for they would swoop down at night out of the darkness on to ranches and camps carrying off everything, from money and horses, to guns and women.

When Madero raised the flag of Revolution up here on the border in 1910 Pancho Villa rushed to join him, not so much because he was interested in restoring the Reform Laws of Juárez—for he was completely uneducated and had probably never even read them—but simply because he hated all wealthy landowners and the clergy. His little band of peasants soon swelled to thousands, and the bandit Pancho Villa became '*mi general*'. Unfortunately, through no fault of Madero's, Pancho

Villa was turned against him; then all he wanted to do was to fight Madero. When he could not get help from the United States he was furious. 'Well, now I hate everybody!' he declared, and rushing from Chihuahua to Juárez on the border he crossed over, and killed everybody he could. The United States, furious, sent a punitive army into Mexico to punish him, but they never caught up with him for he hid with his men in the mountains around Chihuahua.

'From then on,' added Margarita, 'all through the rule of Madero, of Huerta, of Carranza, Pancho Villa succeeded in keeping the whole country in a turmoil. He *was* the Revolution! For a time with his peasant army he was the greatest military power in Mexico.'

'Look, señorita, here is his sword!' His widow handed it to me proudly. The steel blade, made in Oaxaca by a special process, was so fine that when it was detached from the hilt it could be curled round and round to fit into a small box. Inscribed on the blade in Spanish, was the inscription, 'When this snake bites you there is no cure for you!' Even his walking stick contained a thin steel blade that slipped down inside the hollow stick.

Since many people tried to poison him he had a special set of table ware made and used it for all his meals. It was of silver, gold and other alloys that would change colour if there was poison in the food.

At the end of the room was the miniature sculpture of him on his favourite horse, Mile Eater; it had been used as the model for the fine equestrian statue near the station. (This little model had been made in Tlaquepaque, which brought back memories of sitting in the *zocalo* on those old pigskin chairs with William and Bill listening to the *mariachis*.)

Hanging on the wall was Pancho Villa's old banner, embroidered with the words 'Viva la Revolucíon!' and underneath, '1810 Hidalgo–1910 Madero'. Nearby was his old cork helmet, its lining stained and torn, also the revolver which had been in his belt when he was assassinated. He had been ambushed while driving through the streets of Parral; the car, an old grey open

Ford, was out in the yard at the back. Pancho Villa, who had been driving, had been shot directly through the windscreen—ironically enough just when he had finally agreed to retire from his revolutionary activities (with a very generous allowance of *pesos* for himself and his Golden Lads) and was about to begin life as a respectable citizen and landowner.

There were other reminders of the Revolution in Chihuahua too. In the courtyard of the Government Palace we came upon a vivid mural by Pina Mora depicting the last hours of white-haired Father Miguel Hidalgo. The barrels of eight muskets were pressed against his bare chest, and in the background were terrible scenes of carnage—flames and hammers and breaking chains—symbolic of the whole grim history of Revolution. The plaque below read: 'On this spot Don Miguel Hidalgo was shot on the 30th July 1811 at seven a.m.'

It was here in Chihuahua that Hidalgo was held prisoner for ninety-seven days before his execution. When finally he was shot the Spaniards could not get anyone to cut off his head. In the end they had to get an Apache Indian to do it. Four of his lieutenants had been shot with him and the five heads were put in a cart and taken all over the country to be publicly exhibited. The last place they were hung was on the great hooks I had seen on the walls of the fortress-like granary in Guanajuato. The head of Hidalgo was later collected from there and the body from Chihuahua.

Nearby, in a corner of the courtyard, lay a great new bronze bell, waiting to be installed in the tower to replace the present one. It will be this bell which the Governor of Chihuahua will ring in future on every 15th September before he gives the 'Cry of Hidalgo' from the Palace balcony.

It was about two o'clock that afternoon when suddenly there came a long menacing roll of thunder. Swiftly the streets grew dark. Peal upon peal followed till it seemed as if the mountains must be splitting apart. Then, without any further warning, as if a great lake was being tipped up in the sky—down came the rain. Within minutes every dusty street in Chihuahua was a noisy brown torrent. Cars became little islands. their owners peering out like prisoners through the streaming windows. In every shop doorway a little crowd stood staring at the seemingly endless flow of water, while the thunder continued to crash all round us. Then, just as suddenly, it was over; the sky was a brilliant blue again. Were it not for the fact that the sun was now reflected, like a thousand stars, in swirling brown water, you would never know it had rained.

That evening we were invited out to supper by an acquaintance of Margarita's who had once lived in Mexico City but now had a ranch outside Chihuahua. We had met him by chance in the street that morning. Like everyone else in the town he was very excited over the rain.

'You see it is something very special for us in Chihuahua,' he explained. 'Sometimes we can have three hundred and sixty-five days of sun in a year—just like the desert round us. That is why everybody is so excited!'

The restaurant to which he took us was on the outskirts of town —a huge barn-like place with most of the diners in riding boots and wide hats; from the garden outside came the strumming of guitars.

'There are plenty of modern restaurants in the town,' he said 'but for myself I always come here because they serve the real food of Chihuahua.'

On the table were two huge piles of *tortillas*—the usual grey-coloured maize *tortillas*, and others, bigger and whiter which were *tortillas* of wheat. One dish held black beans; in another were different kinds of chile chopped up in oil and vinegar. (Luckily I had learnt the trick of putting salt on my lips to stop them burning after eating a particularly hot piece of chile.) The main dish was *carne seca* (strips of meat cooked by being dried in the sun), something which all the *rancheros* take with them on horseback journeys in the desert since it keeps indefinitely.

'Do tell us something about your ranch,' I said as we sat drinking our coffee.

'Well, for one thing,' he said, 'ranches up here are beginning to be called by numbers instead of names. I run about a thousand cattle—mostly Herefords. I keep the calves till they are nine months old, then export them to the United States in trucks. There they are fattened for about a year in the corn belt of Kansas, then sold for meat.'

'How many acres have you got?' I asked.

'About eighty thousand,' he replied. 'This is a very rich part of the country. Yet it is a sad one too, for it is always sun, sun, sun—never any shade. Except in the mountains, there are so few trees. You *could* plant pines for shade—but then you would get no grass under them, and the altitude is too high for the organ cactus which would make good shade. The solitude is immense up here. I think that is why the people of Chihuahua are very silent. Yet they are very intelligent.' He pointed to two young men in riding boots who had just strolled past. 'You see how thin they are? There is no grease on the cattle here. People eat only lean meat and cheese. All the men's trousers are made with that very short length from the waist because there is nothing to fill them out!'

'Are there many of the original Indians up here still?' asked Margarita. 'It was because of them that my father's family had to leave Chihuahua. We saw one or two in the streets—they looked wild and shy, not like the ones down south.'

'Those were the Tarahumares I expect—there are very few left. When the Spaniards came the Indians up here fought till they were practically exterminated. They were very different Indians from the settled agricultural tribes of the south, like the Aztec and Zapotecs, with their cultures which blended easily with the Spaniards. These in the north were just nomadic hunting tribes, still wild and savage, so the Spaniards colonized this part with those Indians from the south with whom they had interbred. There are just a few of the original tribes left, like the Coras and Apache, and the Yaquis. They are a wild fierce lot! Luckily they live over on the other side of the Sierra Madre Range, a ten days' journey from here on horseback.'

But the main thought in both my mind and Margarita's while we were in Chihuahua was of her father, Jesús Urueta. We spent many hours searching for the house in which he had been born and for the Theatre of the Heroes in which he had given his famous speech for the Centenary of Benito Juárez. Then there had been only the three long streets—Oginaga, Libertie and Independencia. Money came then, as it still does, from cattle and mining, and those residents wealthy enough sent their sons to study in London or Paris.

The house in which he had been born in Oginaga, was now Government Offices; the Theatre of the Heroes had been burnt down, and there were rumours that a cinema was going up on the site. On our last afternoon we sat in the little park which is named after him—the Park of Jesús Urueta—and then went up to the University to see his portrait.

The Director welcomed Margarita warmly—'The daughter of Jesús Urueta! This is indeed an honour!' He sent out for *refrescos*, and afterwards took us across to the University library, where a bronze bust of Jesús Urueta stood on a shelf high above the books, between a bust of Victor Hugo and Benito Juárez.

In an adjoining room hung the portrait of him. Framed in heavy gilt it showed him clad in a white Grecian robe. In his long sensitive hands was a heavy volume inscribed with the single word 'Grecia'. The cloudy sky behind his head held just enough trace of blue to intensify the blue of his eyes which, grave to the point of sternness, gazed directly down upon us. The strong face with its wide intelligent forehead and firm mouth dominated the room. It was a face the like of which you would scarcely see once in a century. It could have been the face of a Plato or an Aristotle. As the librarian pulled the curtains across a little to shut out the strong sunlight, the eyes fixed so intently upon us darkened to a stormy indigo.

I had never seen a photograph of Jesús Urueta, yet the face fitted instantly and perfectly on to the mental image which I had already conceived in my mind and heart. Already I had wished passionately that I could have heard him speak even once. Now I knew that my life must always hold a loss because I had not done so.

This was my last link with Mexico, and the image which I

bore with me next day on the last stage of my long journey to the frontier. As the train carried me nearer and nearer to the little border town of Ciudad Juárez, through the rhythm of the wheels a voice I had never heard was saying in impassioned tones:—

'The great man will be awakened from his sleep and will come again amongst us. . . . And, oh, feeling him at our side, we shall have, like him, our spirit filled with hope, and our eyes fixed upon the stars!'

GLOSSARY

adobe (ah-DOH-bay)—clay bricks dried in the sun
agua (AH-gwa)—water
agua miel—honey water. Sap of *maguey* plant from which *pulque* is made
Ajusco (Ah-HOOS-co)
Anáhuac (Ah-NAH-wahk)—Indian name for Valley of Mexico

Bellas Artes (BAY-as AR-tays)
brasero—portable charcoal stove

cacao (ca-COW)—chocolate bean
calle (CAI-yea)—street
cazuela—pottery bowl for cooking
Chapultepec (Cha-POOL-tay-pec)—Hill of Grasshoppers
charro—horseman in elaborate costume
Chauhtémoc (Kwa-oo-TAY-moc)—nephew of Moctezuma and last Aztec
    Emperor
Chichen Itza (Chi-CHEN Eet-ZA)
chicle (CHICK-lay)—chewing gum
Chihuahua (Chee-WHAR-war)
Cholula (Cho-LOO-la)
comal (ko-MAHL)—iron or clay plate for cooking *tortillas*
corrida (ko-REE-thah)—bull-fight
Cuicuilco (Kwee-KWEEL-ko)—archaic pyramid on the Pedregal

El Tajín (El Tah-HEEN)
enchillada (en-chee-LAH-tha)—*tortilla* cooked in sauce

frijoles (free-HOLE-ays)—beans

Guadalajara (Gwa-dah-lah-HARA)
Guadalupe (Gwa-dah-LOO-pay)
Guanajuato (Gwa-na-HWAR-toh)

hacendado (ah-sen-DAH-doh)—owner of *hacienda*
hacienda (ah-see-EN-da)—big farm with estate
Huerta (HWER-ta)

Insurgentes (Een-soor-HEN-tays)—longest street in Mexico City
Ixtaccíhuatl (Ish-tak-CEE-hwatl)
Ixtapalapa (Ishta-pa-LAH-pa)

[201]

Glossary

Jaime (HI-may)—James
Juárez (HWA-rayz)

Laredo (Lah-RAY-tho)
licenciado (lee-sen-see-AH-tho)—lawyer

machete (mah-SHAY-tay)—long knife used in the fields by the Indians
madrina—godmother at a Mexican wedding
maguey (mah-GAY)—species of *agave* from which *pulque* is obtained
mariachi—street singer
marimba (mah-REEM-bah)—musical instrument like xylophone
masa (MAH-sa)—dough, especially maize dough from which *tortillas* are made
mescal (mehs-KAHL)—distilled alcohol from a *maguey* plant
mestizo (mehs-TEE-zo)—mixed, i.e. Spaniard and Indian
milagros—miracle tokens made from silver or alloy
milpa (MEEL-pah)—small plot of ground, usually for maize
Mitla (MEET-lah)
Mixteca (Mish-TAY-ca)
Moctezuma (Mock-tay-ZOO-mah)—Aztec Emperor. Also spelt Montezuma
mole (MOH-lay)—hot sauce

Nogales (No-GAH-lays)
nopal (no-PAHL)—species of cactus

Oaxaca (Wah-HAH-kah)

Papantla (Pah-PAHN-tla)
Paricutin (Pah-ri-coo-TEEN)—Mexico's youngest volcano
Pedregal (Peh-dray-GAHL)—lava flow outside Mexico City
peón (pay-ON)—worker on *hacienda*
perico (pay-REE-co)—parrot
peso (PAY-so)—smallest denomination in paper money
petate (pay-TAH-tay)—straw mat used by the Mexican Indians for sleeping
picante (pee-KAHN-tay)—hot with chile peppers
Popocatépetl (Po-po-kah-TAY-petl)
posada (po-SAH-tha)—an inn
primo (PREE-mo)—cousin
pulque (POOL-kay)—fermented juice of the *maguey* plant known as the Poor
   Man's Beer

Querétaro (Kay-RAY-tah-ro)
Quetzalcoatl (KAYT-zal-co-atl)—God of Learning and Civilization, etc.

rebozo (ray-BOH-zo)—long narrow shawl worn by Mexican and Indian women
refresco (reh-FRAYS-ko)—refreshment
retablo (reh-TAH-blo)—miracle painting
Ruelas (Roo-AY-las)

[202]

Glossary

San Angel (San ANG-hel)
San Cristóbal de las Casas (San Cris-TOH-bal de las CAH-sas)
San Miguel Allende (San MIGEL Ah-YEN-day)

taco (TAH-ko)—*tortilla* sandwich
tamale (tah-MAH-lay)—maize dough steamed in corn or banana leaf
Taxco (TAHS-ko)
Tehuantepec (Tay-huan-TAY-pec)
Tejeda (Te-HAY-tha)
Teotihuacán (Tay-o-ti-wah-kahn)—Pyramid of Sun and Moon near Mexico
    City
Tenochtitlan (Te-noch-ti-TLAHN)—Ancient city of the Aztecs on which Mexico
    City was built by the Spaniards
tequila (tay-KEE-la)—alcoholic drink made from juice of *maguey* plant
Tezcatlipoca (Tez-cat-li-PO-ca)
Tlaquepaque (TLAH-kay-PAH-kay)
Toluca (Toh-LOO-ca)
Tonalá (Toh-nah-LAH)
tortilla (tor-TEE-yah)—flat maize pancake
Tula (TOO-lah)—ancient city of the Toltecs
tuna (TOO-nah)—fruit of the *nopal* cactus
Tzotzil (Zot-ZEEL)

Urueta, Jesús (Oor-oo-ET-ah Hay-SUS)

Villa Rojas, Dr. (VEE-ah RO-has)

Xochimilco (Sho-chee-MEEL-co)

zarape (sah-RAH-pay)—Indian blanket with slit for head. Also spelt *sarape*
zocalo (ZOH-ca-lo)—square in centre of Mexican town
zopilote (zoh-pi-LO-ti)—black turkey vulture

INDEX

Acapulco, 157–8
Acatlán, 94–5
adobe, 40, 52, 72–3, 78, 129, 145, 150, 154, 164, 171, 189
Aguascalientes, 141
Ajusco, 14, 16
Alvarado 114
Alvarez, Martina Barrios, 63–5
Amatenango, 110–11
Antonio, 29, 70, 74, 76, 78–9, 81–2, 91, 99
Aranga, Doreteo (see Pancho Villa)
Argentina, 49
Arizona, 180, 182
Atl, Dr., 7, 144
Aztecs, 16, 20, 23, 40, 42–3, 46–54, 109, 113–14, 120, 122, 147, 149, 169, 170, 173, 198

Barajas, Joseph, 168
Barogan, Dr. Ignacio, 106
Barragan, Luis, 17
Bellas Artes, 7, 32, 63, 158
Boronova, Irina, 32
Britain, 45
Browning, Robert, 15
Brownsville, Texas, 182
Buenos Aires, 68

Calendar Stone, The Aztec, 53
Canute, King, 45
Cardenas, Primitivo, 140
Carillo, Armando Oliverez, 165, 176
Carlos, 35–43
Carlotta, Empress, 61
Carranza, Venustiana, 67, 195

Caso, Dr. Alfonso, 54, 148, 186
Celaya, 21
Ceneutl, Goddess, 126–7
Ceremony of the New Fire, 43
Cervantes, Miguel de, 161–2, 165–6, 175–8
Chamula, 103–5
Chanal, 107–8
Chapala, Lake, 141–2
Chapultepec, 6, 7, 61
Chatta, 166, 168, 173
Chiapas, 97, 99, 100
Chichén Itzá, 148
Chihuahua, 63–4, 191, 193–9; dogs, 193; University, 191, 199
Chocolate, 31–2, 85, 169–70
Cholula, 51, 150–5
Cinco de Mayo, 60
Coatzacoalcos, 113
Copán, 45
Córdoba, 115–16
Corona, Antonio, 166, 171–2
Corral, Vice President, 66
Cortés, Hernán, 50–1, 113–14, 123, 172
Cuauhtémoc, 6, 51
Cuicuilco, 15, 16, 35, 47
Cusi, Elena, Baroness de Imhoff, 158–9

Davies, W. H., 41
Deneen, William, 107–11, 115, 118, 136–41, 144, 146, 160–4, 167, 169, 172–3, 176, 178, 180, 195
Díaz, de Castillo, Bernal, 47
Díaz, General Porfirio, 62–6

Index

Diego, Juan, 37–8
Don Quixote, 161, 178
Dorres, Sr., 105–7, 110

Eades, Capt. J. Buchanan, 113
El Paso, 191
El Tajín, 45, 119, 126–7

Farrar, Geraldine, 158
Fireworks, 172–3
Fortin de las Flores, 38, 115, 117

Guadalajara, 141
Guadalupe, 36–7, 56
Guanajuato, 146, 160–8, 170, 175–6,
  178, 196; hacienda, the, 163–4,
  168–70; silver mine, the, 173–4;
  University of, 163, 168–9

Harmer, Hilary and Vincent, 193
Hidalgo, Father Miguel, 55, 59, 66,
  168, 195–6
Hospital, Social Security, 155–7
Huerta, General Adolfo de la, 66–7,
  195
Hugo, Victor, 62–3, 199

Ignacio, basket weaver, 145
Ignacio, Saint, 170
Insurgentes, 6, 21, 56–7, 179
Isidro, Saint, 95
Isthmus, The, 111–13
Iturbide, General Augustin, 59
Ixtaccíhuatl, 7, 47, 152, 189
Ixtapalapa, 130

Jaime, 150, 155
Josefina, 75, 76, 78–9
Juárez, Avendida, 7, 68
Juárez, Benito, 59–66, 191, 194, 199–
  200
Juárez, Cuidad, 192, 195, 200

Laredo, 1, 2, 137, 180–1
Latin America Tower, 55–6
Lottery, The National, 55–6

Madagascar, 123
Madero, Avendida, Francisco I, 7, 8,
  62, 68
Madero, Francisco I, 65–6, 194–5
maguey, 39, 40, 122, 129, 148, 154,
  183, 190
Manolete, 54
mariachis, 142, 195
marimba, 96–7, 99, 111, 142
markets, 21–5
Marta and Pepe, 29–30, 32–3, 183,
  191
Matamoros, 180–2
Maximilian of Austria, 60–1
Maya, 45, 148
Mexican hairless dogs, 49–50, 193
Mexico City, 1, 4, 5–18, 28, 32, 71,
  84, 86, 89, 91, 93, 104, 115, 117–18,
  129, 136, 147, 151, 157–8, 180–2,
  188, 191–2
Mexico University, 12, 14, 15
Mexictli, 47
Michoacán, State of, 143–4
milagros, 39, 175
Mina, 11–13, 27–31, 71, 158
Mitla, 183–4, 187
Mixtec, 85, 186
Moctezuma, Don Pedro, 149
Moctezuma, Emperor, 51, 54, 120,
  149
mole poblano, 76–7, 80
Monte Albán, 45, 86, 183–6
Monterrey, 3, 4, 181
Mora, Pina, 196
Morelia, 162
Morelos, Father José, 59
Morran, Charles, 123

Napoleon III, 60, 61
National Palace, 8, 46, 51, 53, 66, 119,
  193
New Spain, 51–2
Nogales, 180–3
nopal cactus, 2, 28, 83, 117–18, 131,
  140–1, 148, 184
Noriega, Dr. Raoul, 53

Index

Oaxaca, 45, 59, 86, 94–7, 111, 183–4, 186–8
Obregón, General Alvaro, 20–1
Obregón, Villa, 20
O'Gorman, John, 14, 16
Olmecs, 45, 153
Orizaba, Mt., 116

Pachuca, 119
Palenque, 45
Papaloapan River, 114
Papantla, 119–27
Paracho, 141, 143–4
Paricutin, 144
Parral, 195
Pátzcuaro, Lake, 144
Pedregal, 11, 14, 16–18, 46, 179
Pedregal, Gardens of the, 17–18
Poinsett, Joel, U.S. Minister, 112
Popocatépetl, 7, 47, 152, 172, 189
Poza Rica, 120
Prescott, Wm. H., 50
Puebla, 60, 150–1, 155, 189
Punitive Army, U.S., 195
Pyramid of the Sun, 41–4

Querétaro, 61
Quetzalcoatl, 44, 50, 148–50

Reforma, Paseo de la, 6, 51, 56, 136
retablos, 174
Rio Grande River, 2, 182
Rivera, Diego, 46, 49–50, 52, 87, 109, 119, 167–8, 193
Rivera, Frieda, 49
Rodin, Auguste, 62–3
Ruelas, Licenciado Enrique, 161–70, 172, 174, 176, 178

Salina Cruz, 104, 113
San Angel, 5, 9–14, 19–34, 58, 118, 136, 146, 158–9, 179–80, 183, 191–2
San Angel, Convent of, 20–1
San Cristóbal de las Casas, 101–4, 108, 111, 180
San Luis Potosí, 139, 141, 181

San Miguel Allende, 136–7
Santa Anna, General, 59
Santa Maria del Rio, 136, 138–9
Saurez, Lopez, 166
Scheffler, Prof. Ernesto, 169, 171–2
Schindler, Wm., 107, 115, 116, 118, 136, 139–41, 143, 160, 162, 166, 169, 173, 176, 178, 180, 195
Sierra Madre Mountains, 97, 98, 140, 198
Siqueros, 10
Steiner, Rudolf, 5, 11

Tarahumare, 198
Taxco, 145
Tecolutla, 128
Tehuantepec, 98–100
Tejeda, Carlos and Mercedes, 159
Tenoch, High Priest, 47
Tenochtitlan, 16, 47–53, 120, 147, 149, 152
Teocali, The Great, 47, 53
Teotihuacán, 16, 35, 41–5, 47, 185
Tepanapa, The, 152–4
Tepexpan, 15
Texcoco, Lake, 47
Tezcatlipoca, 148–9
Tikal, 45
Tlaquepaque, 142, 195
Tloque Nahuaque, 43
Tollan, 42, 147, 149
Toltecs, The, 16, 42, 147, 149, 150, 153
Toluca, 144–5
Tonalá, 141
Totonacs, The, 45, 49, 119, 121–7
Tula, 16, 42, 147–50
Tuxtla Gutiérrez, 97, 100–2, 112
Tzeltal, 105, 110

Urueta, Cordelia, 62–3, 67
Urueta, Edouard, 158
Urueta, Jesús, 58, 62–8, 198–200
Urueta, Margarita, 5, 9, 10–18, 54, 58–68, 70–1, 130, 158, 183, 191, 194–5, 197–9

Index

Valley of Mexico, 7, 42, 47, 131, 152, 183
Vanilla bean, 122–3
Veracruz, 38, 45, 111, 113–16, 119
Villa, Pancho, 193–6
Villa Rojas, Dr. Alfonso, 105, 107–9
Villa, Señora, 194–5

Xanat, Goddess, 122
Xictli, 16

Xochimilco, 22
Xolotl, 49

Yagul, 184, 187
Yaqui, 198
Yucatán, 148, 150

Zacetecas, 192
Zamora, 143
Zapotec, 45, 59, 185–6, 198
Zinacantecan, 102, 103, 106, 107, 112